Arabs Today

Arabs Today

JOEL CARMICHAEL

ANCHOR BOOKS
ANCHOR PRESS/DOUBLEDAY
GARDEN CITY, NEW YORK
1977

The Anchor Books edition is the first publication of
Arabs Today.
Anchor Books edition: 1977

ISBN 0-385-11351-X
Library of Congress Catalog Card Number 76–41554
Copyright © 1977 by Joel Carmichael
All Rights Reserved
Printed in the United States of America
First Edition

Contents

Introduction

The Arabs entered history some thirteen hundred years ago, and have now reappeared. Full of contradictions, they are a group of intense interest. Nowhere is the contrast between the old and the new, commonplace in many societies now coming to terms with modern ideas, more arresting than in the relation between Arabdom and the West.

Even since Europeans descended on Egypt at the beginning of the nineteenth century, the Middle East has been undergoing the upheaval brought about by a torrent of innovations. After transforming the army and administration, modern technology has gone on to disrupt the lives of the huge population of the extinguished Ottoman Empire.

Of course the transformation has not taken place evenly. The upper classes and the intelligentsia have adapted themselves quickly. Having changed both the way they dress and the way they live, they stand out more and more from the rest of the population, still clinging to old-fashioned clothing and rooted in age-old custom.

The range of style in Arabdom is if anything broader than in the West, just because the convulsive changes that have transformed that world have been working themselves out so lopsidedly. The contrast between, say, an oil laborer in Saudi Arabia or an old-style Egyptian peasant and a Beirut graduate of Harvard Business School will seem more obvious than that between an American mountaineer and a Wall Street magnate.

Even more striking than the external differences in lifestyle is the physical variety of the people. If you take a trip from Morocco to Iraq you can depend on seeing quite literally every type of human physique. An examination of the origins of present-day Arabdom will easily account for the immense range of physical appearance.

When the Muslim Arabs poured out of Arabia thirteen centuries ago their military successes gave them access to an endless variety of women. The institution of polygamy bore fruit immediately; slaves bought throughout the known world filled huge harems. Merely mentioning the names of the peoples absorbed by the tide of Muslim conquest and eventual mass conversion to Islam gives one a bird's-eye view of the peculiarly dense mélange that has created more of a "melting pot" than America ever experienced. No ancient people was ever destroyed—genocide, by and large, has been unknown until our own day. Assyrians, Babylonians, Phoenicians, Persians, and Egyptians were not wiped out, but rather took on different identities. Curiously enough, of all the ancient peoples overwhelmed by the Muslims, only the Persians, Turks,

Berbers, and Jews have maintained their identity to this day; the others were all absorbed into the Arabic-speaking masses of the various caliphates and their successor states. Until recently, indeed, they were generally referred to as Saracens and Moors. As we shall see, their awareness of themselves as "Arab" was not to arise until very nearly our own generation and even today has still not been generally accepted.

The handsome descendants of the ancient Phoenicians still inhabit the Fertile Crescent. Their squarish faces, regular features, large eyes, and relatively fair complexions are unmistakable. The great peasant population of Egypt, too, no doubt the most sedentary people on earth, look just like the portraits of ancient Egyptians.

Similarly, though the populations of Persia, Assyria, and Babylonia remained in Mesopotamia and Persia, the overwhelming bulk rapidly acquired Arabic speech after adopting Aramaic speech and becoming Christians or Zoroastrians. The Persians, holding out on their own plateau, were not overwhelmed; their speech survived and emerged once again as the idiom of a nation-state.

Berbers, too, while holding out culturally and linguistically in many parts of Morocco, eventually spoke Arabic. The same goes for the fragments of countless black tribes encountered by Muslims all over Africa and swiftly Islamized.

The remarkable penetration of Africa by Islam, manifest since the initial conquests, has in fact been accelerated since the West opened up Africa in the nineteenth century. While Christianity did not make much headway among the blacks, perhaps because of its emphasis on monogamy, or simply because it was an appendage of invaders, Islam could benefit by the pacification of the continent by Europeans and through a more or less "organic" network of traders and businessmen. Often marrying local women and settling down, they could make the advantages of Islam as a world community available to uprooted and disaffiliated natives. Arabic speech itself spread, and even when Arabic itself did not become a vernacular, it became the learned language of the tribes or sections of tribes converted to Islam.

This is to say nothing of the additions to the mélange made by the short-lived influx of Crusaders. A shepherd from the Hauran in Jordan, for instance, may well turn up looking exactly like a Scottish highlander.

Thus, on meeting an "Arab" nowadays it will be impossible to say in advance what he will look like —tall, blond, and blue-eyed? "Semitic"? Snub-featured, wiry, darkish? Tall, slender, black? In short, the motleyness of the far-flung populations now lumped together as "Arab" cannot be overemphasized. More than a hundred million people—statistics for many countries are more than vague—they are divided in twenty countries. All the countries belong to the Arab League, founded at the end of the Second World War, and all are members of the United Nations.

The area taken in by the entire panorama—from Morocco on the Atlantic Ocean to Iraq on the borders of Persia, from Syria in the north to Yemen in the south of the Arabian Peninsula—is about five million square miles, almost two million more than the United States.

The terrain, to be sure, varies widely: the Sahara

Desert, itself well-nigh three million square miles, protrudes into the Arabic-speaking belt of countries in North Africa, extending substantially into Algeria and Morocco and constituting practically the whole of Libya. Egypt itself is no more than a narrow strip of habitable land along the Nile River —the "gift of the Nile" indeed; 97 per cent of the country is a desert, though not so forbidding as the Sahara. Of the one million miles of the Arabian Peninsula, the core in the center is a barren steppe, though again not so forbidding as the Sahara. All these wildernesses, including the Sahara itself, can of course be restored to cultivation by irrigation; the vast oil resources of the Persian Gulf make the desalting of the sea quite feasible.

The Fertile Crescent, by contrast, well deserves its name; with running streams and lush farmlands, it is a genuine granary. In the whole of the Fertile Crescent, indeed, only the State of Israel seems disadvantaged. There is a popular saying that when the angel Gabriel was carrying on his back two great bags of rocks to distribute to the whole of the world, one of them split open as he was crossing the Holy Land. This is paralleled in our day by the wry Israeli remark that in his wanderings Moses was hard put to find the only spot in the Middle East where there was no oil whatever, or the older Jewish saying that if only Moses had staggered on a little longer he might have wound up among the marvelous greenery and waters of Lebanon and Syria.

Perhaps the chief oddity about Arabdom is that so little is known about it. This is strange not only because Arabs made a titanic impact on history when they first became historically significant, but also because Arabic-speaking peoples, spread along the southern shores of the Mediterranean and concentrated around the eastern Mediterranean and the Persian Gulf, have remained at the hub of the world's activities ever since. One would think that there was enough substance here to stimulate curiosity about such an assembly of populations dispersed over such an enormous area. Moreover, such an assembly of people should have a special interest for one sixth of mankind—the Muslims. The origins of the Muslim religion itself, as well as the language in which it is expressed, should lend the Arabs special luster.

Yet for centuries there was little interest in the Arabic-speaking population of the Middle East and North Africa. Playing an obscure role as perhaps the least interesting of the peoples governed by the Ottoman Empire, they made a blurred impression on Europeans. They were seen as one of two stereotypes: either as gallant knights of the desert, appealing to the European love of glamour, or as hereditary villains, a vestige of the early Middle Ages when to agonized Christians it seemed that Christendom itself was on the verge of being overwhelmed by a new force thrusting itself out from the Arabian Desert. This feeling was later softened, or complemented, to be sure, by the efflorescence of great cultural centers in the vast Islamic world. There, in Baghdad, Damascus, and Spain, the arts and sciences were elegantly cultivated at a time when European civilization was at its lowest ebb.

In the modern era, this notion of the gallant sheik, inherited from the mysteriously glamourous world of medieval Islam, has been counterbalanced by the equally unrealistic notion of Arabs as furtive and disreputable—filthy, feckless, futile. Thus in popular literature, and even more so in that great new pastime of the twentieth century, the movies, readers and audiences might expect Arabs to be played by Rudolf Valentino or Douglas Fairbanks or to be portrayed as an assortment of rascals and ruffians in adventures laid against exotic backgrounds.

It is safe to say that in all these mythological constructions, which either kindled the imaginations of romantics or repelled the man in the street, no truly human traits were discernible. The reality of the lives of tens of millions of people was almost wholly disregarded, except by the handful of English explorers, themselves uniformly romantics, who began penetrating the hinterland of the Middle East at the end of the nineteenth century and the beginning of the twentieth, partly as agents of empire and partly in a sentimental quest for evidence bearing on the origins of Christianity.

It is true that toward the end of the nineteenth century, scholarship was stimulated by the seemingly limitless wealth of material—cultural, historical, religious—to be found in an investigation of Islam. In Central Europe, France, England, and Russia, scholars began plowing up the initially stony terrain of past history; they began excavating, reorganizing, and reassessing our knowledge of the Islamic past, indissolubly linked, as it turned out, with the medieval past of Europe itself.

Braving the lush complexity of the Arabic language, these scholars re-created part of Islam, giving it shape and intelligibility, at a time when Muslim scholarship was for all practical purposes nonexistent, and thus fleshed out a whole new di-

mension of world history. The ramified civilization
that had assimilated Persian and Greek culture, and
become in its turn another channel for the heritage
of classical Greece, was thus unearthed, rein-
terpreted, and exported, oddly enough, to the heirs
of the Muslim past for their own edification.

Yet despite scholarly studies, modern Islam was
bound to remain alien to ordinary outsiders. Overwhelming in both past and present impact, it is a
source of bewilderment. The fact that Islam takes
in a sixth of mankind is no more than a dim abstraction, which in the case of Arabdom is complicated,
moreover, by the further abstraction, equally dim,
of the function of Christians in Arabdom. Numerically, to be sure, Arabic-speaking Christians are
only 10 per cent of Arabdom, but since they have
had greater contact with Europeans and Americans
it is only natural to overestimate their importance
in their own countries. Also, since Arabic-speaking
Christians have played a disproportionate part in
the political activity of the post-World War II period, this conspicuousness is perhaps itself a natural
reason to assign them a special role in the contemporary Middle East.

In particular, since Christians historically have
been the seminal influence in the formation of modern Arab consciousness, it is natural for outsiders
to be perplexed by their true role in the various
countries of the Middle East. Very often far more
"nationalistic" in contemporary movements than
Muslims—who in the back of their minds remain
anchored in the matrix of cosmopolitan Islam—Arabic-speaking Christians often strike outsiders, at
least, as more vociferously "Arab," very curiously,
than the Muslims themselves.

All these problems of definition and identity, of course, have been endlessly exacerbated in our own day. All Islam, from Southeast Asia and the Indian subcontinent to the shores of the Atlantic Ocean in North Africa, has been churned up. The penetration of Islam that began a couple of centuries ago has been bursting out in all directions, as the breakneck assimilation of Western technology has been accompanied by the rapid growth of an elite to implement it.

The flooding of Western universities by Muslim students, on the heels of the Arabic-speaking Christian migration to Western cultural centers that began during the nineteenth century, and the establishment throughout Arabdom of academies, colleges, and universities modeled on Western institutions, have brought about a remarkably dense cultural borrowing on a vast scale. The export of Western technology throughout the world has been accompanied by Western culture as a whole— elites everywhere have absorbed Western culture in the broadest sense, even at a moment when countless specific features of that culture have been rejected or even prohibited. At the very moment that elites throughout the world are dependent on the culture of the West, the import of Western ideologies (as in Mao Tse-tung's "adaptation" of Marxism) has been accompanied by a rejection of Western influence in other domains, such as literature.

Since the end of the Second World War, of course, the attention of the Western world has been turned, somewhat reluctantly, perhaps, to the inner evolution of Arabdom because of the conflict with Israel. Since a few years after the Second

World War, Israel has served as a rallying point for the countless tensions, frictions, and rivalries through the eastern Mediterranean and North Africa. Involved in the penetration of the area by both the Soviet Union and the United States, Israel had now maximized the critical sensitivity of the entire area so as to make it, in the minds of many, a powderkeg.

It might have seemed, at first glance, that the conflict with Israel was so trivial, from the Arab point of view, that it was incapable of creating any real fervor. If proportions are taken into account, an outsider might well have been prepared to shrug it aside. Why, one might think, should such a vast community get so inflamed by a dispute involving a strip of land no more than ten thousand square miles?

Yet the fervor grew: The hostility of neighboring governments to the anchoring of a Jewish community in the former mandated territory of Palestine attained fever pitch; with the establishment of the State of Israel in the spring of 1948, in the wake of an abrupt evacuation of British forces, that hostility crystallized in a full-dress though somewhat lopsided war. Five Arab governments—Egypt, Iraq, Syria, Lebanon, and Jordan—refused to accept either the cumbersome, defective partition arrangement voted by the United Nations, still less the emergence of an independent Jewish state, and launched a full-scale attack on it.

The factor of morale proved decisive; against seemingly great odds, the infant state managed to hold its own and even occupy some additional territory. Since then Israel has not only failed to pacify its immediate vicinity, but has also served as a rallying point for nationalist sentiment throughout the Middle East—indeed, throughout Arabdom as a whole.

The steady growth of hostility to the State of Israel tells us that it has deep roots in the psyche of the elites, if not of the "masses" of Arabdom. It is plain that national consciousness, ripening however sketchily in the countries bordering Israel, has been inflamed by the presence of what is felt to be an alien community. To Arab nationalists the lands so recently inherited from the Ottoman Empire seem naturally destined for integration in larger entities.

Arab national consciousness has been stimulated, moreover, by the presence of the relatively highly educated Arabic-speaking inhabitants of the former segment of Mandatory Palestine west of the Jordan, now ruled by Israel. The presence of Arabs from Israeli territory in neighboring countries, including several hundred thousand refugees from the warfare of 1948 who have not been absorbed, has served as a further point of crystallization in the obdurate rejection of Israel by its neighbors.

Internally, on the Israeli side, the conflict with Arabdom produced a vast crop of Jewish refugees —well-nigh a million—from all parts of the Arab world. Almost half the Jewish population of Israel is "oriental."

Externally, the presence of numerous well-wishers of Israel in the United States has further stiffened the American stance in the Middle East, which is already considered crucial by American opinion because of the massive deployment of Soviet influence throughout the area. The historic sponsorship by United States administrations of the State of Israel since 1948, in its turn resting on the official sponsorship of Zionist aspirations since the First World War, has created the present-day framework of events in the area—a seemingly intractable hostility on the part of the neighbors of Israel, plus the exploitation of that hostility by the Soviet rulers.

And in the past generation, beyond the byplay of national interests, perhaps the crowning paradox of the Arab nationalist movement—the revival of Muslim religiosity—has been looming up larger and larger.

Though preceded into national consciousness by Arabic-speaking Christians, the Arabic-speaking Muslims who became Arab nationalists naturally remained Muslims. Simultaneously Muslims and Arab nationalists, they have lately become militants both as Muslims and as Arabs—a combination that harks back, curiously enough, to the period of genesis when Arabs alone were Muslims. Thus, beyond all the frills of secularism, the renaissance of Muslim fervor may again overarch Arabdom.

Most recently, a cardinal factor has emerged that may shape events not only in the Middle East but also throughout the world. In Western imagination Arabdom has suddenly been endowed with boundless economic power—oil has changed the world.

It was only in the autumn of 1973 that the new state of affairs burst in on world consciousness with staggering force. Though the presence of oil in the Middle East had been known since long before World War II, and though the oil kingdoms and oil principalities around the Persian Gulf had been accumulating huge cash reserves since then, it was not until 1973 that the accumulation of liquid funds, and at the same time the resolve of the Arab leaders to use them for political purposes, finally combined into a stunningly effective weapon.

The cash reserves in the hands of the oil producers of the Middle East have transformed the curiosity of the world at large about the Arabs. Oil has given a novel dimension to the attention they are now enjoying. More than 60 per cent of the world's proven oil reserves are located in the Middle East, mostly around the Persian Gulf; the cash flow resulting from the sale of oil has achieved astronomical dimensions. Thus the indispensability of oil for the industrial world and the political squeeze implemented by the oil boycott of 1973 have been spliced together. Many people are justified, plainly, in the speculation that we may be on the threshold of a historic tilt in the balance of world power. Matchless quantities of cash are now in the hands of a new economic entity, and even if there may be substantial difficulties in investing these funds in the local economy, the oil producers themselves have acquired a tremendous lever for influencing the play of economic forces throughout the world.

It is entirely possible, to be sure, that the preponderance of the "oil weapon" in its nature will be short-lived; indeed, the awareness of that must surely account for the decisiveness with which the oil producers concerted their forces in 1973 and since: They are plainly determined to maximize the revenues from oil in order to bring themselves closer to an industrial status that in the long run is essential for power as well as affluence. The knowledge that on the one hand the oil reserves must eventually give out, while on the other that the development of alternative sources of fuel is being frantically promoted by all nations with advanced technologies, has concentrated Arab political action precisely because the scope of the oil weapon is so restricted. In the space of another decade the relative effectiveness of the oil producers of the Middle East will have sharply declined, perhaps vanished, as the industrial countries of the world regroup and apply their collective brainpower to the development of alternatives to oil. Mankind, no longer dependent on the windfall of fossilized fuels, will have to create self-perpetuating forms of power.

Yet for the time being, the Arab oil weapon represents the intrusion of a new factor in the complex of forces governing our planet. And the thrust of that factor cannot be assessed without a survey of its agent—the Arabic-speaking world of today.

Time Line

1254–1517   Mamelukes rule Egypt.

1258   Hulagu captures Baghdad; end of the Abbasids.

1453   Conquest of Constantinople by the Ottoman Turks.

1492   Moors expelled from Spain.

1517   Ottoman Turks conquer Egypt.

1543   Turks conquer Hungary.

1686   Turks lose Hungary.

1740   Muhammad ibn Abd al-Wahhab in Arabia.

1783   Catherine the Great of Russia conquers the Crimean Tatars.

1798   Napoleon in Egypt.

1881   French occupy Tunisia; British occupy Egypt.

1897   First Zionist Congress meets (in Basle, Switzerland).

1914–18   First World War.

1915   The McMahon correspondence with Hussein, sherif of Mecca, promises support for an Arab state in Middle East, in return for help against the Turks, allied with the Central Powers.

            Sykes-Picot Agreement between Great Britain and France, giving Palestine (including area east of Jordan River) to the British sphere of influence.

1917   Balfour Declaration proclaims a Jewish National Home in Palestine.

1920   British conquer Palestine, also Baghdad. Turks surrender. Palestine and Iraq put under British; Syria and Lebanon under French.

1922   British Mandates approved by League of Nations.

1923   Turkey becomes a republic.

1924   Caliphate abolished; Ibn Saud conquers the Hijaz.

1929   Riots in Palestine against Jewish National Home.

1933   Hitler comes to power in Germany; Jewish immigration to Palestine begins increasing.

1939   British suspend Jewish immigration and land purchase. Zionist militants fight British blockade on immigration.

1939–45   Second World War.

1944   French Mandate ends in Syria and Lebanon; they become independent.

1945   Arab League formed in Cairo through British initiative. Charter of United Nations signed.

1946   Trans-Jordan becomes independent (known as Jordan after April 1949)

1947   United Nations Special Committee on Palestine recommends partition of Palestine (without Jordan). Accepted by Jews, rejected by Arabs.

1948   British end Palestine Mandate. State of Israel proclaimed. Arab states (Egypt, Jordan, Lebanon, Syria, Iraq) attack.

1949   Cease-fire between Israel and Egypt; armistice between Israel and Jordan, Lebanon, Syria.

1952   Monarchy abolished in Egypt; Gamal Nasser sets up new regime.

1956   Suez Canal nationalized. War breaks

	out between Great Britain, France, and Israel on one side, and Egypt.
1958	Iraqi monarchy abolished by army junta.
1962	Algeria becomes independent, followed by Tunisia and Morocco.
1964	Palestine Liberation Organization formed.
1967	War breaks out between Egypt, Lebanon, Syria, and Jordan on one side against Israel. Israel wins: occupies Sinai Peninsula, the West Bank of the Jordan, the Gaza Strip, and the Golan Heights.
1973	Egyptians and Syrians attack Israel: repulsed.
1975	"Shuttle diplomacy" of Henry Kissinger produces disengagement in Sinai. Civil war in Lebanon.
1976	Lebanon shattered; Syria establishes *de facto* protectorate.

I

Genesis of a People

The past of the Arabs has special importance, to them and to others, because it is rooted in the creation of a world religion—Islam. Some thirteen hundred years ago Islam welded together the great tribes of the Arabian Peninsula, turned them into a people, and made their language the vehicle of a new civilization.

Yet, though Islam shaped the Arab people and changed the world, it was paradoxically the handiwork of one individual—Muhammad ibn Abdallah, a merchant in the long-distance import-export trade of the great Bedouin tribes whose camel caravans, carrying commodities of all kinds, shuttled between Syria, Persia, and Egypt.

Muhammad was, it seems, stricken by a melancholic crisis around the age of forty. Increasingly preoccupied with the meaning of life and, more particularly, with what was going to happen to him on the Day of Judgment, he began questioning the Jews and Christians he encountered on his long

business trips. The information he got from them
was a little distorted, it seems, by the defectiveness
of their knowledge, the quirks of tradition, and by
Muhammad's own selectivity; he made use of it,
however, in the trances he began falling into, in
which, he reported, the angel Gabriel conveyed to
him what he was to put down and transmit to his
people "in the noble Arabic tongue."

Thus the Quran—"recitation"—is an assembly of
the revelations made by God via the angel Gabriel
to Muhammad, which Muhammad was to convey
to his people in their own language. It is the only
sacred book of a major religion actually composed
by one individual.

Muhammad himself dictated each segment the
moment it came down to him; after his death some
private collections were made, which were superseded a couple of decades later by an official edition.

Muhammad took over the fundamental element
of Israel's faith—the belief in one God. Indeed,
throughout the beginnings of the Quran, Muhammad harps on the role of Moses, though Muhammad dropped the special role of Israel as Partner of
the One in a special Covenant and replaced it with
a unique role for himself as the Final Envoy of the
One. Since it was Muhammad who had the insight
to perceive the weightiness of Moses' message, it
was he who bore the responsibility for it in his own
day. Muhammad, as the last of all the other prophets of the past who had variously conveyed to mankind the message of the one God, was the "seal" of
the Prophets. After Muhammad—no one. Islam,
similarly, as the consummation of all previous
codes, simply canceled them.

Muhammad conceived of himself, accordingly, as the tail end of a long line of Jews—Abraham, Isaac, Jacob, and, perhaps a little surprisingly, Jesus. Muhammad did not know Jesus was supposed to be the Son of God but simply considered him his last predecessor.

By the time Muhammad appeared, all major religious groups (notably Christians and Jews) had revealed books. By providing his countrymen with such a book he immediately put them on the same level as other religious communities, indeed, still higher, since the Quran, the definitive book, was naturally seen to supersede all other books, just as Muhammad himself superseded all preceding prophets.

Muhammad held his message to be obviously truthful just because it agreed with that of earlier prophets—that is, the pillars of the Old Testament, Abraham, Isaac, Jacob, and Moses; in its turn he considered his message to be nothing more than an excerpt from a celestial book, sections of which had been translated by God himself into idiomatic Arabic.

Muhammad did not claim that he had actually read the celestial book; Allah had simply selected those portions of it he wanted Muhammad to convey to his people via Gabriel. Consequently, in case there were any serious differences between what he said and what earlier prophets were supposed to have said, the differences could only have arisen through willful neglect or even falsification by Jews and/or Christians.

For Muslims the Quran is unique—it is thought to contain everything. It is the chief miracle of Muhammad's life; its very existence demonstrates its miraculousness. Its uniqueness is shown by its prophesying of future events; its reporting of past events that would otherwise remain unknown; the failure of all attempts to rival it; and above all, by its very texture. Muslims generally say that its style, its musicality, the utter perfection of its diction, its syntax, its vocabulary, and all else about it demonstrate that uniqueness beyond question. (Non-Muslims generally have different reactions; Muslims who may not agree keep silent.)

Though the sacred books of Judaism and Christianity are also, in principle, wholly authoritative, individual oddities can be discussed and taken to indicate human fallibility in the transmission of God's word. In Muslim theology, however, the literal divinity of the Quran was laid down long ago and became an actual dogma some centuries after Muhammad; he came to be thought of as a mere tool of Allah, chosen to transmit a text that Muhammad himself had to be taught to understand. His sole relationship to the text, accordingly, was seen as that of guardian—he had to keep the divine word perfect. Thus what was in Christianity somewhat exceptional—such as when Christian theologians sometimes insisted that even the punctuation of the Hebrew Scriptures was divinely inspired—was the rule in Islam. Any criticism of the Quran, even from a formal point of view, came to be forbidden.

Countless generations of Muslims, especially those whose native language was Arabic, have treated the Quran with limitless reverence. It has been popular to tuck all sorts of tags from the Quran into any kind of poetry or prose: Lines from it were extensively made use of as ornamentation; miniatures were painted with a Quranic background.

Muhammad's creation of the Quran was a remarkable feat. Though the great Arabian tribes had somehow worked out—just how remains mysterious—a poetic dialect understood throughout the peninsula, nothing had ever been written down except inscriptions. The Quran marked the beginning of something entirely novel: Muhammad, using a form of rhymed prose—inimitable, like all else in the Quran—contrived expressions never used before. Thus the Quran was the very first work of prose in Arabic, and has remained the standard ever since.

The reverence accorded the Quran has had the no doubt understandable consequence of making it a magical instrument in spite of Muhammad's explicit prohibition of magic (5:92); it is even considered to have medical effectiveness. Traditional sayings like "the first Sura has a remedy for every disease" abound in Muslim tradition. Its actual text had thus been used to make amulets and talismans, included as part of the phraseology of incantations and in numerological divining, and in divining based on the first lines encountered at a random opening of its text. These ancient magical techniques, inherited like so much else from the Hellenistic world (itself the heir of ancient magical rites and devices), are rife throughout Islam.

MUSLIM DOCTRINE

At the time of the rise of Islam, Arabian pagans were too sophisticated—perhaps, like Muhammad, through contact with outsiders—to be satisfied by

the various forms of animistic fetichism that made
up their religion. Feeling menaced by the Fire to
Come, they sought protection. No doubt Muhammad's personal distress corresponded to this general
concern. The central preoccupations of Christianity—the notion of salvation conveyed by the
redemptive immolation of a Deity and the sacra-
ments bound up with it—were unknown to Muhammad and his early followers, and have remained
intellectually unintelligible to the Muslim community ever since.

The early Muslims seem to have shared the
primordial impulse of Jewish monotheism—to learn
what God was and what he wanted from people.
Thus, though Islam later came to incorporate
Greek philosophy, Roman law, and Persian ideas of
the state, its focal doctrine, like its Judaic model, is
simple.

Summed up in a couple of sentences, it might,
indeed, seem too exiguous to provide the foundation for a major religion:

> Believe in God and in his Envoy, in the Book he
> sent down to his Envoy and in the Scriptures he
> sent down beforehand. Whoever denies God, and
> his angels, and his books, and his envoys and the Fi-
> nal Day, has strayed a long way from the Truth
> (Qur. 4:135).

It is evident from Muhammad's theory of his
own spiritual antecedents, and particularly from the
constant references to Moses in the earliest parts of
the Quran, that Muhammad's notion of the Deity
was wholly dependent on the religious experience
of the Jews. Islam re-created Jehovah, altogether
autocratic, supreme—the Unique Almighty bound

by nothing. At the same time God, though independent of and in a sense indifferent to man's concerns, is also seen as supremely compassionate. This is what makes him accessible to man's needs. Yet God must choose to be approachable before anyone can approach him; he sends astray and sets straight whomever he wishes to (Qur. 7:178).

This is the sum total of Muhammad's theology.

The notion of God's arbitrary decision, made independently of personal conduct, may have been inherited from Gnosticism (in its turn it was taken over by Calvin and others). Omnipotence, plus capriciousness, led Islam, perhaps more than Judaism and Christianity, to the somewhat inhibiting idea that laws of nature—that is, regular concordances rooted in the nature of the world—really do not exist at all, but merely seem to be there because it suits Almighty God to go on allowing them to seem so; that is, apparent causality is in reality the Almighty One's habit. The simplicity of this formulation heightens the starkness of the dilemma arising out of the conflict between the old idea of virtue being rewarded and vice punished and the sheer absoluteness of God's will. Muhammad never cleared this up; he was not, perhaps, aware of it as a problem.

In its simplicity, doctrine shifts the emphasis of life to behavior, again as in Judaism. In Islam, traditionally borne on five pillars—the profession of faith ("There is no god but God, and Muhammad is his Envoy"), communal prayer, almsgiving, the pilgrimage to Mecca, and the month-long fast of Ramadan—doctrine is far outweighed by actions.

Cultural content, too, consisting of Muhammad's two contributions—the idea of One God and its expression in a book—is almost equally simple. Beyond the proclamation of Divine Unity and the endorsement of himself as the Seal of the Prophets, Muhammad made only a few simple additions, which were also borrowed from Judaism—some of the kosher laws, a condemnation of alcoholic liquor, and, most important, rules of conduct. Modeled, in theory, on Muhammad's actual life, these rules were structurally very similar to the Jewish "Halacha," a body of prescriptions incorporated in the Talmud that in their ensemble cover practically all aspects of daily life.

This idea had arisen among the Jews, it would seem, as a way of uniting the many Jews scattered throughout the Middle East, North Africa, and Europe after the destruction of the Jewish State by the Romans in A.D. 70. While settled in Palestine, the Jews had celebrated their religion in the manner of other peoples, but in exile they found it necessary to articulate the conditions of their uprootedness in a body of rules encasing all life within a framework of divinely sanctioned law. A hundred years after the dispersion of A.D. 70, for instance, Jews were studying the details of the Temple service in Jerusalem in a form that had never been practiced even when the Temple was in existence. For a people dispersed the emphasis on religion, and more especially on the ritualization of religion, was felt to be a necessary and more or less effective substitute for collective life in a settled homeland. The oddity is only how this artificial idea could have been taken over by a free people living normally on its own lands and free of any need to straitjacket its spiritual life.

Muhammad must have been impressed by his

Jewish informants, whoever they were; or perhaps he was temperamentally disposed to this form of programming. In any case he made the Judaic Halacha the germ of what in Arabic came to be known as the Shari'a, a body of rules that structured Islam. It is this overriding idea of the "correct" life that anchors Muslim constitutionality in the divine sanction required for all administration.

Thus, looked at globally, Judaism had an enduring effect not merely on Muhammad's initial inspiration—Moses' message—but also on the manner in which he and his first successors assimilated the Jewish idea of confining all personal as well as collective behavior within the framework of specific prescriptions ascribed to God. Since this lends importance to what would otherwise seem to be trivialities, life as a whole becomes enhanced by a ritualization that reaffirms the sacrality of the world—everything is plunged into the glow of the eternal.

Politically, of course, this militates against change, since God's order, instituted by his Envoy, must perforce be stable. Change must be seen as a return to the purity of the beginning, in contrast with the corruption of the present period. Change must be justified as really the *correction* of change.

THE QURAN AMPLIFIED

In Muhammad's lifetime Allah was supposed to be governing his believers directly; afterward the Quran had to be looked to as the repository of all Allah's major injunctions. It consequently served as the basis of the sociopolitical as well as the religious order. But to the Muslims the distinction between these two orders is, in theory, inessential. Islam claims to encompass everything, to fuse every single aspect of life, every moment of the day and night, into a seamless web expressing the divine will. Thus prayer as well as taxation, meals, and international law, every personal and collective activity is supposed to be molded by Allah's will as revealed to Muhammad.

The Quran, which can be roughly broken up into categories, is the basis for all legislation: Its three primary subjects are doctrine (covered by a word meaning the unity of God), histories (of previous prophets), and law. Put somewhat differently, the Quran covers three stages in Muhammad's public career. The first details his preoccupation with the Day of Judgment (while still in Mecca he was wholly in the grip of this idea). The second is a form of "prophetology": It discusses previous "envoys" of God who had the same message. The last (corresponding to Muhammad's move to Medina) treats social organization and law, touching a little casually on politics, daily problems, and so on.

On the other hand, since the Quran was manifestly inadequate—if only because of its brevity— as a legal code or political handbook, and for that matter as a religious statement, it had to be built on. As a result it was thought necessary to collect separately every single thing Muhammad was reported to have said or done in his capacity as a mere man —that is, when he was *not* supposed to be expressing Allah's will. In the Quran, too, an obvious distinction is made between Muhammad's statements as Envoy of God and his mere talk as a human being. If Muhammad's own example could not serve as an authoritative model, his companions were looked to; if they did not serve, the next generation could be researched.

This process had begun even toward the end of Muhammad's life: When two Muslims met, one was supposed to ask for news (*hadith*), whereupon the other would narrate something to do with Muhammad. After Muhammad's death the word *hadith* was applied to anecdotes and tales that were no longer new; it came to mean, in fact, tradition, a foundation for practically all aspects of life. By the middle of the ninth century A.D. a huge mass of "tradition" had been accumulated in this way.

(The formula guaranteeing the authenticity of a given tradition was a simple one: If X said something about Muhammad to Y, and Y told it to the chronicler, and both X and Y were sound, the transmission was accepted as authoritative.)

Hadith came to be regarded as superior to the sacred book; in practice the usages of the faithful could not be counteracted even by references to the book itself. In this way the growing community evolved a method of securing both the authoritativeness of divine sanction and the pliability of *ad hoc* measures contrived to cope with life's contingencies. Since Muhammad's miraculous powers were taken for granted—and indeed, believed in more and more as orthodoxy solidified—he could be ascribed any number of predictions to fit into the conditions of a later age. There was nothing, of course, to forestall the composition of pseudo-anecdotes; during the following centuries, in fact, all differences of opinion could find, or claim to find, support for any current interest. Thus divine authority could have all the appurtenances of continuity.

The supplementation provided by *hadith* was paralleled by an additional supplement based on the exegesis of the Quran itself, since in theory any thing at all, *a fortiori* any theological or political movement, could be found there and indeed had to be. Thus textual study went far beyond the mere explanation of obscure or contradictory sections; interpretation followed explanation.

Interpretation, could, of course, mean practically anything. The "plain" meaning of a text might be considered subordinate to an "inner" meaning; by taking a variety of allegorical, numerological, or other starting points, practically anything could be read into or out of any text whatsoever, all this without seeming to be departing from the text itself.

It need hardly be recalled that the above process is a very exact copy of what the Jews had gone through with respect to the Torah, which, like the Quran, had very soon been paralleled by the "oral" law, of the same value (according to the Pharisees) as the written text. Here too text was subjected over the ages to interpretation, in order to squeeze an endless variety of life situations into the same phraseology.

THE SPREAD OF ISLAM

As recorded in the Quran—a very personal book —the intensity of Muhammad's dread about the Final Day, which stamps its earliest sections, seems to have diminished. The deep anxiety that had afflicted him was removed from his immediate horizons by the active life he embarked on as a result of the energy derived from his initial visions. In any case, in the space of only a few years he shifted to the notion that since the world was manifestly continuing, after all, the great thing was to settle its affairs in a coherent and meritorious manner. At the very outset of his career, in short, Muhammad accomplished what it took Christianity and Judaism an entire epoch to overcome—the idea of the imminent World's End, which had inspired St. Paul as well as Jesus.

Grappling with the real world inevitably involved Muhammad in politics. Initially alienated as he was from his fellow Meccans, he found it natural to approach the Jews, who had been roving about Arabia for generations and settling in dense and often prosperous communities. From his point of view they were, so to speak, already converted.

Muhammad seems to have expected them to follow him automatically. His approach was simple; he said, in effect: "Since I am only bringing the message of Moses, why don't you accept me?" They inverted the syllogism by replying: "If all you are doing is bringing us the message of Moses, why do we need *you?*"

This led to a falling out: Muhammad expropriated and slaughtered the substantial Jewish community near Medina, and soon forbade the presence of any Jews in northern Arabia. In the Quran he made both Jews and Christians inferior to Muslims.

On the other hand, from what may be called a general Jewish point of view, there was nothing at all repellent in Muhammad's original message, at least before he reintroduced paganism into Islam via the pilgrimage to the Black Stone (the Ka'ba) in Mecca. All he had asked the Jews to do, after all, was to accept him as the Final Envoy with the message of the One God.

It seems likely, therefore, that the reason for the falling out between Muhammad and the Jews, which had such fateful consequences for them in Arabia itself and later on throughout Islam, was partly the potent factor of economic envy. The landholdings of the Jews, often affluent cultivators, were simply confiscated as booty by the successful Muslim Arabs. Perhaps a still more relevant reason was that the specific Jews imitated by Muhammad were themselves sectarians, "Karaites," who rejected everything later than the Hebrew Scriptures (the Talmud, too) and were resented by orthodox Jews.

This conception of Muhammad as the Final Envoy bearing the ancient message that God had already revealed through many other messengers to many other peoples—recorded by Islamic tradition as numbering 124,000!—collided at once, also, with Arabian paganism. However, Arabian paganism was not at all a coherent body of beliefs or practices; it was never articulated, still less equipped with a philosophy. By the sixth century A.D. it was crumbling, no doubt because of Jewish influence as well as from contact with many individual Christians in the towns and commercial centers of the peninsula.

In Muhammad's lifetime the deserts of Arabia, as well as the few oases scattered throughout the million square miles of the peninsula and the few towns that served as trading and religious centers, were dominated by the great Bedouin tribes. They roved about the far-flung pasture lands with their camels, the only animals that could sustain the long treks and thus give their masters command of their environment.

The great tribes were seldom at ease with each other; raiding and skirmishing were the rule. On the other hand, warfare was seldom serious; it would never be the objective of a Bedouin foray to kill anyone, but simply to seize camels, sheep, or horses. Killing was a serious matter; it could be revenged only by further killing. Vendetta was the governing principle; indeed, the Old Testament prescription of "an eye for an eye" was strongly in effect. The shared code essentially softened tribal behavior.

Coexistence was further promoted by the existence of the poetic dialect common to all the tribes throughout the peninsula and even northward wherever they had penetrated. It was this poetic dialect, and the love of language it illustrated and furthered, that provided the bickering tribes with a common culture of some complexity. They were further unified by a common pagan cult centered in Mecca, where a trinity of pagan deities had been worshiped for ages.

At first sight Muhammad's chances of making any impression on the great tribes might have seemed minimal. The pagan Arabs were essentially indifferent to religion, their chief pursuits being wine bibbing, womanizing, and the amateur warfare attendant on skirmishing with and raiding other tribes. Their ideals may be summed up in the word *muruwwa*—the Arabic equivalent of manliness, which was the same for them as for the ancient Romans, Greeks, and other pagans. Thus Muhammad's concentration on the Day of Judgment, buttressed by his emphasis on the One God, might have seemed an obstacle to success.

But his organizing abilities proved formidable;

adapting his new views to the tribal organization of the peninsula, he created, in effect, another tribe—the tribe of his followers.

Unwelcome in Mecca, Muhammad was forced to flee; his flight to Medina (the starting point of the Muslim calendar) marked the beginning of his worldly career. Initially a private visionary, he became a political organizer. Counterposing his new group first to the Jews living near Medina, and then to the pagan tribes, he succeeded in expanding the realm of his own "tribe" by both conquest and persuasion, and finally made an alliance between his own followers and the great tribes for a joint enterprise—the conquest of the surrounding world.

It is not quite clear whether Muhammad really thought of himself as preaching his ideas to the Arabians alone or to mankind, but the course of events after his death made it obvious that the natural tendency of Islam was to expand. It was so successful that the notion of Islam as being in principle at war with the world until the world gave in was institutionalized very early on. One of the chief duties of the Caliphs, the title taken by Muhammad's successors, was to expand the territory of Muslim dominion, though this was never, to be sure, accompanied by the notion of enforced conversion except against pagans. In the case of Persia, it was decided, after some hesitation, to let the Persians into the community of those who held a revealed book by including Zoroastrianism as a monotheism (in the teeth of the evidence).

Muslim law does not accept, in principle, the idea of Islam living at peace with unbelievers, even though it may be unavoidable for given periods of time. In theory *jihad*—the Holy War against those outside Islam—must remain the ideal of Muslim rulers until all men are Muslims. Nor is it the ideal of rulers alone—Islam as a collectivity is considered to bear within itself the need to conquer the world, since it is the Muslim community as a community that is conceived of as the locus of faith. If authority in Islam came from God, the corollary was obvious—there could be no equality between those who have the benefit of God's commands and those who don't. Because of this, Muhammad granted Jews and Christians a degree of legitimacy —they had, after all, a sacred book whose essence he agreed with. To be sure, if they did not accept him, they were to be second-class citizens vis-à-vis the believers, treated somewhat humiliatingly, subject to a special tax, and kept out of the army and in theory out of the state summits. But the people with no sacred book at all—the pagans, or the overwhelming bulk of mankind—were confronted by a simple choice: conversion or death.

Muhammad was familiar with conditions in the north of the peninsula, particularly Syria, as a result of his import-export trips; other Bedouin notables, equally cosmopolitan because of their livelihood, were also knowledgeable about the sedentary societies of Persia, Syria, and Egypt. Moreover, the political circumstances of the Byzantine Empire that ruled Egypt, and of the Persian Empire that ruled the whole of the northern Arabian peninsula as well as Mesopotamia, were exceptionally favorable to Bedouin penetration.

The Egyptian elite felt itself to be oppressed by the narrowness of the Byzantine Church; the population was in a state of simmering discontent. This was also true in the Persian Empire, where the peasantry, generally Christians speaking Aramaic (a language akin to Arabic and felt, somehow, to be the same), was heavily exploited in the classical manner by the Zoroastrian upper classes.

Once united, the Bedouins proved to be a factor substantial enough to upset the balance prevailing between the Persian and the Byzantine empires. In only a few years, through the deployment of probably no more than a few thousand troops, the Muslim warriors installed themselves with scarcely any armed resistance as rulers of the Fertile Crescent—comprising Syria (with Lebanon and Palestine), Mesopotamia (including present-day Iraq), Egypt, and the coast of North Africa as far as Spain. In the space of eighty years, indeed, the Bedouin conquests assembled an empire covering an area larger than the Roman Empire had managed to accumulate in the course of eight centuries.

Thus in the first wave of Bedouin conquest the Middle East, North Africa, and Spain were conquered. The tide was stopped at Tours by Charles Martel, and from then on receded to some sort of stability at roughly the present area of Arabic speech. Later on, when Islam was taken up by the Turks and Tatars, it was to have varying fortunes throughout Asia, especially India, until its stabilization in the eighteenth and nineteenth centuries with the notable expansion, and later decline, of the Ottoman Empire.

Wherever they penetrated, the Bedouins were perforce a tiny minority, and highly vulnerable. They could never have maintained their sovereignty at all if they had not had the support, either active or passive, of large sections of their subjects.

In Mesopotamia and Syria, including Palestine,

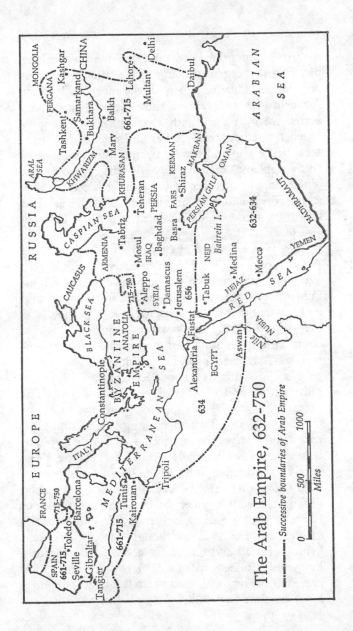

The Arab Empire, 632–750

- - - - Successive boundaries of Arab Empire

the Arabs, superimposed on the Aramaic-speaking peasantry, merged quickly with the indigenous population. This happened all the more easily since for centuries beforehand these peasants had been accustomed to deal with two buffer states, governed by sedentarized Arabs and intended to protect the Persian and the Byzantine frontiers, respectively, against the pressure of the great tribes. These populations simply became Arabized without strain; they adopted Arabic and thus became, at that time, more or less identical with their Bedouin overlords.

In Persian areas and in Central Asia, however, the Arabs soon lost their identity. Intermarrying freely via polygamy with the native populations, the Bedouin upper crust was soon assimilated biologically and for that matter linguistically.

In Egypt, too, the peasant population, whose composition has remained undisturbed for millennia, was Arabized only in speech, and later on in religion. To this day real Bedouins can be found only within and on the edges of the desert. The urban elite was heavily infused with the blood of the long series of Turkic-speaking rulers from Central Asia; hence the aspect of the urban population varies substantially from that of the peasantry, still the great bulk of the population.

In North Africa, the racial situation was again different. Bedouin rule, during the first phase of Islam, was constantly troubled by an endless series of Berber revolts. Even though the Berbers kept being defeated and ultimately accepted Islam, for a long time (indeed, to this day) they retained their national identity and even their language as well as some institutions and habits. When Arabic was finally accepted, all the dialects received a characteristic North African stamp, no doubt a hangover of the original Berber languages.

THE MYTH OF MUSLIM FANATICISM

In the West it very soon became a cliché that this huge area was conquered by religious fanatics determined to impose their faith on the infidel. It is a cliché that has been current for thirteen hundred years and is still commonly believed, even by Muslims.

Yet nothing could be farther from the truth. It was not merely that the Bedouin Arabs were not pious at the start, but also, as we can see from the rationale of the conquests, and more particularly from the manner in which the Arabs ruled their new territories, the last thing they were thinking of was religious conversion. This is evident if only from the length of time it took for the populations of Egypt, Syria, Iraq, and the Fertile Crescent to become Muslim.

At the outset the new faith could hardly have seemed at all novel. It was, after all, no more than a basic affirmation of the unity of God in essence, the same monotheism professed by both Judaism and Christianity. Thus it might have seemed natural for many Egyptians—uniformly Monophysite, believing in the single nature of Jesus Christ—to accept the new faith without much ado. So it was also for the Aramaic-speaking peasantry of Syria and Mesopotamia, who felt kinship with the Bedouins from the start. In addition, since non-Muslims were subjected to a heavy tax (justified in theory by the mere fact of their being non-Muslim), they had still another incentive to become Muslims.

In general it may be said that all nomads have had the same ambition when conquering sedentary populations. They want to act as "herdsmen" to them. Just as nomads are content to survey their flocks producing milk and meat and vigorously multiplying, so they generally avoid interfering with their subjects beyond forcing them to pay up. Nomads are never despotic in any other way—they are indifferent to religion, local customs, culture, and indeed anything that might hamper their taxation. Bedouin rule may be said to have rotated around a simple principle: squeeze!

Hence Islam, whose faith, on the positive side, was acceptable, and on the negative side, brought financial hardship to those who did not accept it, might have been thought to lead very rapidly to the assimilation of new subjects.

Yet mass conversion was not to take place for three generations or more. The Bedouins had so little interest in persuading their subjects to embrace their creed that there was, quite simply, no way for anyone to *become* a Muslim. There was no ritual for entering the Muslim community, no *rite de passage*, no mechanism whereby a nonbeliever could formally become a believer.

Arab hegemony was so taken for granted, it seemed so obvious to the earliest generation of Muslims that Islam was, so to speak, the personal chattel of the Arab tribes, that the only way to join this universal faith was to get into one of the Bedouin tribes first—to join the tribe in order to join the universal community. The tribes, after all, had survived—they had not lost their identity by becoming partisans of Muhammad; they had simply, as tribes, associated themselves with Muhammad's "tribe" of believers—from now on all equal in Islam. Since the outsiders could not get in at first except via the tribal structure, they gradually, then in droves, became "clients" (*mawali*) of one Bedouin tribe or another.

Thus becoming a Muslim, during the first decades of the conquests, involved slipping into the exclusive milieu of the snobbish Arab aristocracy. The first Caliphate, propped up on the taxes squeezed out of the subjugated rabble, simply used its position at the summit of the new society to preserve the exclusiveness of the parvenu aristocracy.

But it was incapable of maintaining its ethnic integrity. The universal implications of Islam—embedded, after all, in the Holy Quran—could not be circumvented. People could not be *forbidden* to become Muslims. The notion of a social grouping based on blood had been replaced, in principle, by Muhammad's notion of the religious community; that notion was now applied to non-Arabs.

Thus, even though at the outset religion had been the exclusive prerogative of the Arab aristocracy, it was also the channel by which more and more outsiders could insinuate themselves into it.

For a while appearances, so to speak, could be kept up: As outsiders joined the Arabian tribes in increasing numbers, genealogies were fabricated wholesale. But the numbers involved soon made this impossible. Converts streamed into the new Muslim cities, run at first as military encampments; their place was taken by the hordes of Bedouin still pouring out of the peninsula to share the rewards for the invention of Islam. These Arab newcomers had nothing to do with the conquests themselves; hence their presence in the conquered territories, together with the mass infiltration of foreigners into Islam, soon threw an intolerable strain on the fiscal structure of the state.

The treasury of the first Muslim state was dependent almost entirely on the Bedouin notion of taxation—making the subjects pay the way for the rulers. The head tax levied at first on all non-Muslims—mainly, of course, the Christians of the Middle East and the Persians—was enough to sustain the state entirely. Though the head tax could be avoided by the simple device of becoming the "client" of a tribe and so joining the Muslim community, it is obvious that in the long run this practice could not be sustained. How could people be kept out of Islam? The device of imposing Arabian clientship on converts, whether or not it was consciously intended, could in any case act as no more than a stopgap. As the subject populations of the Middle East learned Arabic, it was only natural for the overwhelming bulk of them to make the slight further transition and, having become Arabic speakers, to become Muslim believers. By the end of the first century, the great bulk of the Middle Eastern populations had become professing Muslims; the finances of the state had been thrown completely out of kilter; new sources of income had to be found.

Thus the initially race-conscious conquerors were swamped by a flood of converts to their own beliefs. The economic benefits of Islam had proved so great that the Arabs were eventually shouldered aside by peoples their religion made it impossible to exclude.

Islam, the very instrument that made the Arabs a world force, also submerged their nationality. Having welded the Arabs together as a people, Islam prevented them from becoming a nation. Coming onto the world stage as the banner bearers of a new faith, the Arabs were to be submerged by the consequences of their own success. They were not to surface again, as a people, until our own day.

ISLAM—A NEW WORLD ORDER

Islam created a vast community that came to define itself, much like medieval Christendom, in terms of religion. This was just what entailed the elimination of the Arabs as rulers. The first century of Islam saw a profound and well-nigh unconscious conflict between the secular dominion of the great Bedouin tribes and the universal, leveling tendencies inherent in Islam as a religion. The Arab aristocracy was in fact undone by the socio-economic implications of its prize possession—Islam.

Within only a few generations after Muhammad —roughly 125 years—conversions to Islam were taking place en masse: Mass fraternizing in Islam brought about an unprecedented crossbreeding. The legacy of the original Muslim Arabs—the Arabic language and the rudiments of a new religion—could now be taken up by other, more civilized peoples, who fleshed out the skeleton of the original faith with their own culture. Once they had accepted Islam and Arabic, their cultural superiority could be implemented. The Hellenic East overrun by the Muslim Arabs was, after all, infinitely superior to the Bedouins in all the arts and techniques of civilization, to say nothing of sheer numbers.

This blanket process was accentuated by three factors. During the era of the conquests, the theory of the state was anchored in the rootlessness of the Arab aristocracy; Arabs were forbidden to own land in the conquered areas outside Arabia. The whole of the society was milked as a unit; taxes were paid into a central treasury and then distributed among the aristocracy. But when the abolition of the head tax on non-Muslims shattered the foundations of the treasury, new methods of taxation had to be improvised.

The situation was exacerbated as Arabs kept pouring out of the peninsula in pursuit of pickings. As the revenues of the central treasury diminished, these propertyless Arabs following in the wake of their conquering kinfolk could be accommodated only by allowing them to settle in the empty parts of the conquered territories; in its turn this inevitably transformed them into petty farmers—peasants with no aristocratic pretensions. Anyone with a farm or business had to pay taxes regardless of who he was. Thus these Arab newcomers merged with the peasantry throughout the Middle East.

Third, the Arabs were obliged to take over the entire bureaucratic structure of the conquered countries—a structure that was itself the heritage of the ancient East inherited by the declining Hellenistic civilization and handed on in its turn to its most recent overlords. In so doing, the Arabs inherited the absolutist summit of the bureaucratic apparatus as well as the ancient oriental despotism.

This process reinforced the extrusion of the Arabs as a ruling caste. It gave the Islamic state another leveling tendency. As the evolving state structure concentrated authority in a despotic apex, all classes of the population were leveled indiscriminately down to a grade infinitely below the despot. The prince among the Bedouin Arabs who had previously been in both theory and practice no more than the first among equals—an expression of the primitive democracy that had always been the primordial feature of Arabian society—became an old-fashioned oriental despot profoundly inimical to the Arab aristocracy.

In this way the straitjacket of the bureaucracy debased both Arabs and non-Arabs equally under a unique sovereign. As the leveling tendency dredged up recruits for the bureaucratic apparatus from all strata of the population, the prestige of the former governing caste of Arab aristocrats was rapidly obliterated. Their successors could present themselves without self-consciousness to the world at large, no longer as Arabs in any but a remote and often fictitious genealogical sense, but as Muslim rulers of an Arabic-speaking Muslim society.

To sum up the above epigrammatically: The Arabs came out of the desert as exclusive English gentlemen, rigidly exclusive, indifferent to the life of "native" society, and squeezing the indigenous population for the maintenance of a military establishment. In the course of exercising dominion, however, they found themselves transformed into "French humanitarians"—the bearers of an ecumenical ethic that destroyed their temporal dominion and replaced it with the richer fruits of cultural assimilation. Their language became the idiom of many millions of speakers in a lush civilization. The leveling tendencies of Islam destroyed Bedouin exclusivism for good. By dissolving the Arab tribes and laying the foundations of a flexible and essentially democratic society, in a hybrid Arabic-speaking community entirely distinct from the original Arab tribes, it created a new world.

The traditional view, still held by many, that the religion of Islam was forced on people at the point of a sword is now generally admitted to be merely fatuous. What was imposed was something that at first was quite different—not the faith of Islam, but its dominion. Thus the remarkable results of Bedouin Arab colonization, which steeped whole peoples over unparalleled distances in the Arabic language and eventually in the religion of the Arabs, were not at all the results of a brutal military policy, but the consequences of an unforeseen and perhaps undesired socio-economic process.

On the surface the social and cultural transformation brought about by the Arab colonization was striking. In A.D. 600 Greek, Coptic, Latin, Aramaic, and Persian were being spoken in the Middle East and North Africa; Christianity and Zoroastrianism, with countless churches, temples, monasteries, and shrines, were thriving in North Africa and Persia, respectively. Only a few centuries later, Arabic had become the vernacular or *lingua franca* in North Africa and the vehicle of ideas and of the state in Persia, while Islam blanketed the whole of the homogenized society. A unitary civilization was manifest.

Yet that unity had been created not by Islam itself, strangely enough, but by the conquests of Alexander the Great a millennium before. It was paradoxically Hellenism that provided Islam with a cultural core and an arena for expansion and growth even during the modern era. The unity established by Hellenism had been camouflaged by the multiplicity of languages and cults. Islam brought it to the surface.

The integration of the Muslim Arab conquerors from the peninsula into the cultural patterns of the Middle East was signalized by the transfer of the capital of the first Caliphate, Damascus, the headquarters of the House of Umayya—an Arab dynasty—to Baghdad, the new capital of the House of Abbas—a Persian dynasty—125 years after Muhammad.

The extinction of Arab predominance in the new Islamic state gave the word "Islam" a meaning that was quite distinct from the worldly dominion of an oligarchy of Arab magnates more or less indifferent to religion. It became the label for the reincarnation of the old Persian state—a universal, unitary civilization in which the Arabs were merely one among many, with only their language and some elements in their religion remaining to indicate their role as midwife to a new entity.

When the Arabs proper—the great Bedouin tribes—retired from an executive role in the state a few generations after creating it, the peoples they had been exploiting stirred mightily. The Persians, notably, setting up their own form of national self-expression within the Islamic state, spearheaded the anti-Arab reaction. This in its turn had the effect of increasing and deepening the religious feelings of the Arabs themselves; vis-à-vis the cultivated peoples they had conquered, their religion and their language were the only distinctions they could claim. Since the language was now the common property of a vast and motley population—the Persians, for that matter, were quick to demonstrate how much better they knew desert idiom than the Bedouins themselves!—it was natural for religion to be enhanced by way of compensation.

In the beginning the Arabs had shown an almost total lack of proselytizing zeal; the process of conversion was in fact now carried on by the new converts—Arameans, Greeks, Persians. Since the Arameans had previously been familiar with clericalism, and the Persians with notions of a state church and the ubiquitous diffusion of religion, this added the final touch to the resurrection of the pre-Islamic state—a state ecclesiastical hierarchy.

With the establishment of this hierarchy it became an occupational interest, so to speak, to convert the infidels, in sharp contrast with the indifference of the previous aristocratic, nonclerical state of the Arabs. The process of conversion was also furthered by the base the despot now found in a class of people that among the Arabs had never existed at all—the learned scribes. Abetted by the enforced equality of all under the aegis of the absolutist oriental state, these learned scribes could operate among the masses of the people with a religious zeal entirely beyond the capacities or interests of the Arab aristocrats. For this reason religious motivations, quite secondary during the period of Arab ascendancy, reasserted themselves in the now different conditions of the Islamic melting pot. By the third and fourth centuries after Muhammad, the expansion of Islam had already attained its present proportions.

These massive developments pivoted on one factor—language. The Arab Muslims had no need to learn a foreign language, nor any interest. As rulers they could expect the population to produce, at first interpreters, and then, with the succeeding generation, native speakers. Moreover, the language of the Holy Quran had to be Arabic; the piety of the new faith insisted on the uniqueness of the language as the vehicle of the religion. (Indeed, no Muslim translation of the Quran was made until the twentieth century, when Turkey dropped the Arabic script and translated the Quran into a Latinized Turkish.)

The notion that a language is somehow the hallmark of nationality—a banality for the modern age—was not to become current for centuries, not until the formation of nation-states in Western Europe epitomized by the spread of the principle of nationality in the wake of the French Revolution.

In this way Arabic, detribalized, became the vehicle of a vast new civilization. The motley effect of the Arab world today—its medley of races, colors, and types—reflects the great ingathering of cultures and peoples a thousand years ago.

If one could imagine the Roman Empire going into decline after having spread Latin to all its subject peoples, who then a millennium later tried to reconstitute themselves a unit, one might have an idea of the great variety confined within the same cultural mold that Islam, and more particularly the Arab world, presents to the outsider's eye today.

For more than a thousand years, the forebears of the peoples that in our own day were to emerge as "Arabs" were contained in the bosom of this global society, a densely integrated compound of language, religion, law, and institutions.

II

An Old/New Empire

The horizons of the new Muslim world empire, beginning around A.D. 800, were capacious. The empire was a vast pool, with many currents merged in a torrent of creativity that at the time and for many later epochs was unique. Under the aegis of rulers with no spiritual interests of their own to speak of beyond religion and perhaps poetry, it was possible for the ancient cultures of the Middle East to fuse into one superculture.

There was complete freedom of communication throughout an unprecedentedly large area. Scholars were at home everywhere in Islam; functionaries might serve one prince or another. Political divisions were overlaid by a common awareness of cultural homogeneity. Sects themselves, even though they generally had local roots, or links to specific social strata, were international in scope.

Soon, only a few generations after the conquests, the initially simple ideas of Islam had been extended, enriched, and complicated by the intellectual abilities of the subjugated nations—principally the Persians, then the Aramaic-speaking Syrians from the Fertile Crescent and the Greek-speaking and Coptic-speaking inhabitants of Egypt, as well as the great Berber tribes of North Africa.

GREEK AND PERSIAN INFLUENCES

The main component of the new "Islamic" civilization was Greek. The entire heritage of Greece —both of ancient, classical Greece and of the Hellenistic culture that had prevailed in the Roman Empire and survived in Byzantium—was taken over lock, stock, and barrel. All the works of the standard Greek authorities—pre-eminently, of course, Plato and Aristotle—were translated *en bloc* and served as the foundation of Islamic thought, just as later, in the early Middle Ages, they would serve in the renaissance of European culture. This process was obscured for a long time by the hostility of the Roman Catholic and Greek Orthodox churches to the pretensions of Islam. Though at the outset Islam had seemed simple enough to be well-nigh acceptable as a version of monotheism, as soon as Christian thinkers became properly aware of it, they denounced it as a "heresy." Because it was expressed in a difficult language written in strange characters, the notion that Islam was essentially "different" quickly gained currency (and survives, indeed, to this day). Even at the moment when medieval philosophers were borrowing freely from Arabic translations of Greek classics—very often mediated by Jews translating basic texts into Hebrew, which were then translated into Arabic to be transmitted to Europe via further Latin translations—Islam was felt to be "strange."

Yet the scholarly activity of the past hundred years has made what was obvious even in the beginning still more so. Arabic became, essentially, a channel for the transmission of Hellenism.

Hellenism made three intellectual contributions to Islam: basic concepts, principles of classification, and the systematization of thought through abstractions. Even the strain of mysticism brought by Islam as its earliest gift was articulated in exclusively Hellenistic terms. The most intimate experiences of the Muslim's mysticism could be systematized, curiously enough, only in the tools provided by Christian predecessors. The lives of the Sufi saints, for instance, are quite simply modeled on the Greek *Lives of the Philosophers;* not only is the preoccupation with courtly love expressed by the same Hellenistic literary apparatus, but also the whole idea of the originality of the poet, indeed the theory of imitation itself, is drawn from Greek models.

Hellenism provided Islam with much new subject matter for reflection. Hellenism's vast assembly of factual data was absorbed by the Muslims, who then, of course, made their own contributions. Many of the new concepts were drawn predominantly from medicine and the natural sciences, which, during the preceding centuries, had been developed throughout the Aramaic-speaking area as well as to some extent in Persia. Greek political ideas also served the Muslims, who could use Greek political science to transcend the mere ethical studies of the ancient Persians before advancing on their own.

Generations later, when Islam was pressed hard by the Crusades, and concentrated on orthodoxy as a barrier to sectarian dissolution, emphasizing its own traditions in an attempt to confine philosophy to a subsidiary domain, Hellenism had already established itself as unshakable. Intellectually, Islam was now constituted by its Hellenistic component; the camouflage of a common tongue, deceptive to the outsider, was ultimately irrelevant to its cultural content.

A similar dynamic applied to the Muslim assimilation of Persian culture. The Muslim Arabs simply took over the immense riches of Persian historiography and religiosity and translated them into the new medium.

The work of translation was easily accomplished. In the space of a generation or two, countless Aramaic-speaking subjects of Islam joined Persians and Egyptians in translating endlessly from Greek and Persian. A new elite soon sprang up. Arabic, assimilated in the space of a generation and now a mother tongue, was simply filled up with knowledge inherited from other cultures. The Arab Muslim rulers, for their part, had no objection. In fact, after two generations of inbreeding with the women of the subjugated populations, a new community had evolved, different in kind from the indolent elite of the peninsula.

The leaders now ruled a vast population fused under the umbrella of a single state, a single language, and increasingly a single religion. Having mingled the ideas of the Greeks and Persians and established a vast mercantile community encompassing an unprecedentedly large area, the Muslim Arabs might legitimately claim to have created the first successor to the world state of the Romans.

SCIENCES AND ART

Since Islam represents the fulfillment of God's will on earth, from the Muslim point of view the state exists not merely to serve the needs of the community in general but to make sure that its *right* needs will be accommodated. Essentially, those right needs simply consist of the service of Allah, which is seen as the only way to attain true happiness. The paramount function of the state, accordingly, is to ensure the correct worship of God.

In theory, then, the function of the state is ethical: The individual believer, who is called upon to "command the good and prohibit the bad" (Qur. 3:100), is protected in doing so by the state, which with the same end in view also protects believers not only from schism and heresy, but also from the non-Muslim world. The state exists primarily to provide a framework for the fulfillment of all the prescriptions for the good life as laid down by the law that stems from the sacred book.

The transmission of the law itself is, of course, the affair of theologians, who are—much like rabbis —essentially no more than responsible for systematizing and interpreting the law. Such lawyers are indispensable to the state if only because they are essential to the very survival of Islam as a God-shielded community. And if the individual believer is to lead the right life, as of course he must wish to, he too is bound to remain part of Islam—the believing community.

The key role played by theology in Islam also

affects the attitude toward science, which is not supposed to exist for its own sake, nor is it conceived of as a way of glorifying God.

Science in Islam was split up into "Arabic sciences"—the investigation of Muhammad's life as preserved in the sources—and the ancient sciences, which are supposed to encompass natural sciences, investigating the nature of "the world."

The reason science had to begin with an inquiry into the actual materials that constituted revelation lay in the ambiguities that invested the earliest text of the Quran. When a couple of decades after Muhammad's death in 632 the attempt had been made to root out the "private" editions of the Quran, not all variants had been affected. In addition, the script in use at the time allowed for some ambiguities, not only in the text but also in the actual vocabulary, to say nothing of the ideas. This made lexicography indispensable; it was the beginning of the "Arabic sciences" and was based, in the event, on the matchless wealth of pre-Islamic poetry.

While literature was eventually to become a more or less autonomous subject, it was bound to be affected as a classical discipline by the reverence extended to the revelations for which it served as medium; hence the classical language *as such* acquired an aroma of sanctity. This was true, no doubt, partly because in a basically illiterate milieu there was something sacred about writing. Once the revelations had been written down, their sacrality, so to speak, was reinforced.

The same prestige was shared, of course, by the traditions concerning Muhammad, which had evolved by necessity to fill up the gaps inevitably left by the brevity and lopsidedness of the Quran. The savants accepted the study of philosophy and literature because they were obviously indispensable to the study of *hadith*. In this way, grammar and lexicography, and for that matter the doctrine of rhyme, came into the orbit of religion as auxiliaries to the study of the sacred tradition.

Since tradition was necessarily adapted to current sociopolitical needs—indeed, as we have seen, it came into existence for just such reasons—it was naturally subject to the exigencies of both theology and politics. Traditionalists produced a variety of biographical collections, all used in the establishment of various political and/or theological attitudes. Theology was also systematized, assembled, sifted, and interpreted, and Canon Law was molded out of a body of *ad hoc* administrative decisions and precedents anchored in local usages. Thus it was integrated into a theological system and became, in fact, the cardinal Islamic science.

The roots of this theological systematization were four: The first, of course, was the Quran itself; the second, the tradition recalling the Prophet's conduct as a man; the third, consensus (of the learned); and the fourth, reasoning by analogy (where all else has failed). This altogether fundamental Muslim science had to be analyzed by a special body of experts; it was a specific area of jurisprudence whose criteria had to be ultimately derived from the primacy accorded the unchallengeable facts of faith.

The outside world came next: That too was considered worthy of inquiry only because it was necessary for the community to orient itself properly in order to be able to perform its primary function of ensuring the proper worship of God. Thus scholars began to study geography when the executive had to find out something about the territories it found itself governing; the early Muslims had conquered so much so fast that they knew next to nothing about enormous, complex areas. History was studied not only for data touching on the life of Muhammad but also in order to single out the right basis for legal and religious precedents. Similarly, for the well-being of the believing community, some thought had to be given to administration, the theory of taxation, and the very organization of the community itself—that is, the government. Such needs gave rise, naturally, to all-encompassing theories of political science as well as to a doctrine of institutions.

Mathematics and astronomy also were naturally indispensable for establishing the right direction for praying, as well as for the management of the calendar, which because of its religious function was also sacred. Medicine was an obvious practical necessity.

Theoretically, however, anything that went beyond these basic necessities was superfluous. This explains the air of caprice, the slight suggestion of rootlessness, that may seem to surround the role of science as a whole in Islam. Despite the contributions to the natural sciences actually made by Muslim scientists following in the footsteps of their Greek masters, despite the interest shown in the sciences by the government itself, and despite the fashionable enthusiasm sometimes aroused in educated people, neither the sciences nor their practical applications seem to have struck proper root in Islamic society. They always remained somewhat

contaminated, as it were, by the feeling that they
bordered on what truly pious people had no business doing; from a strictly orthodox point of view
they distracted attention from the authentic believer's concern.

Hence the Muslim contributions to medicine and
mathematics were in areas somewhat beyond the
orthodox milieu, where specific scientists could be
daring enough to apply themselves. Interest in the
natural sciences as well as in philosophy tended to
be restricted to rather obscure circles; ultimately
the work of would-be scientists was frustrated or
forgotten, not necessarily because of actual
conflicts with orthodoxy, but rather because of
their own feeling that there was no social appreciation of their work. For instance Muslim writers
in Arabic and Persian who discussed the distribution
of the various orders of the animal kingdom were
generally interested not in a zoological description
but in their theological purpose. Consequently, as
Islam began systematically declining in the later
Middle Ages, and scientific enterprise for all practical purposes became extinct in the Muslim world,
the decline had no particular effect on the ordinary
Muslim. His world view was indifferent to it.

This no doubt explains the passive sense of won-
der a Muslim inquirer might feel when confronted
by the mysteries of God's handiwork. Instead of
the impulsion to thought that so many Greeks un-
derwent as they struggled to grasp an element of
the natural order, their Muslim successors, even
when inspired by Greek writings, generally did not
get beyond a sort of naïve stupefaction at the fact
of the mystery.

Though Greek dialectics, metaphysics, and psychology, together with the theology of the Greek Orthodox Church, enabled the Muslims to formulate and defend their faith within a doctrinal structure, the fact that revelation had to be elaborated within a philosophical doctrine did not have the effect of implanting philosophical inquiry as such on Islamic terrain. Most of the positions borrowed from Greek thought were simply digested by speculative theology and turned into props for the exposition of the faith. Hence philosophy never became as fundamental as it had been in classical antiquity.

Philosophy in classical antiquity had been able to treat all questions, including the postulates of religion, and had ranged from cosmology and metaphysics to ethics and politics. In fact, philosophy in the Hellenistic period was no longer even in competition with religion; it was beginning to replace it —in many milieux it already had—and had, in any case, become the basis of real education. In Islam, philosophy remained subordinate. Since the paramount verities were considered to have been long since established, there was no scope for philosophy as far as those were concerned. Since revelation was considered beyond intellectual control, with theology as its chief safeguard, there was simply no room in fundamental matters for philosophy at all.

This applied, naturally enough, to the sciences too. In view of the primacy of revelation, the certainty of scientific knowledge necessarily had to be denied. In an extreme formulation it was stated that prophecy was manifestly possible because forms of knowledge existed for which reason could not conceivably have been responsible, such as in medicine and astronomy. Such knowledge was dependent on nothing but divine inspiration and assistance unattainable by observation. Since some astronomical laws are based on phenomena that might take place only once in a thousand years, how could these be personally observed?

Accordingly, no philosophy could be acceptable that did not safeguard the primacy of faith. Philosophy concentrated on logic, which could be used for theological speculation, and on physics, psychology, and metaphysics. In Islam, theology never sought for intellectual vindication of faith in the manner of Augustine and Thomas Aquinas, for whom rational cognition, *where possible*, was held to be superior to cognition through faith.

Hence philosophy never became entirely integrated with Islam, which it could have become only by taking revelation for granted somehow as an indispensable prop to reason. Philosophy never freed itself sufficiently to deal with the concept of the creation from nothing, nor was it any help in trying to turn the notion of the world's end—which remained part of Islam—into a coherent picture of reality.

As in the modern world, philosophy in Islam became essentially a speciality, but one that was never thought to be of any interest to nonspecialists. It was not included in the two basic categories of Muslim education, the humanities and the sciences, neither of which required any philosophical training at all. Cultivated only by a handful of theologians and some philosophers proper, and occasionally by laymen or eccentric scholars, it was considered somewhat esoteric. Its alien origin was a perpetual mortgage on its acceptability.

Though literature achieved a vast growth, it dis-

tinguished itself variously in different domains.
Writers paid no attention to two of the three
genres developed in antiquity—drama and epic—
but rather regarded poetry as the pinnacle of verbal
art, primarily, perhaps, because it calls for so much
more skill than prose.

The Islamic public has always admired the virtu-
osity with which the rules of prosody are handled;
traditional forms have always been revered, and in-
novation frowned on. The ode must have an un-
varying reference to bygone love at the beginning;
the poet is then obliged to get on a splendid camel
and set out to brave the hazards of the desert; he
must wind up with a request to some notable, by
lauding his tribe on himself, or by speaking on behalf of some group with respect to some public
matter. Down to the beginning of this century, indeed, the pagan tradition—equated with the classical—had been the most potent single strain in
Arabic poetry, though some Persian innovations
(notably some new meters and the banqueting
songs) as well as Hellenistic tendencies (with some
novel behavior in love) came into it along the way.

Oddly enough, even though the foci of Islamic
civilization from the very outset have always been
the great urban centers, the whole of Arabic literature has been colored by the quasimystical glamour
of the desert and the ideals of Bedouin society. Because of the prestige inherent in the life of the
Bedouin, principally on the theory that the Quran
itself could best be understood through the "pure
classical" speech of the great tribes, a tincture of
lyricism derived from the ecstasy of the desert kept
recurring throughout Arabic poetry.

Later on, to be sure, with the emergence of a

Persian style of life only partially veiled by the new
garments of Islam, there was a flowering of poetry
that conveyed the glamour of court life, together
with a playing up of a subtle, romanticized form of
love that was to pass into the European heritage via
Spain and the troubadours. Always potent even in
the desert, where it was indeed the chief channel of
ideas as well as a weapon of warfare, poetry became an instrument of politics. Unbridled laudation
and equally unbridled satire, together with the restrictions imposed by accepted conventions, re-
sulted in a sort of competition that eventually reduced the real content of poetry to its own
ornamentation.

Indeed, verbal perfection was always preferred
to originality, a concept never very attractive to
Islam. At all times, even at the zenith of creativity
in the Arabic language, and *a fortiori* after the systematic decline that began eight hundred years ago,
the continuity of forms was piously promoted. A
poet was not, in fact, expected to be original; his
talent was assessed by his style of embroidering a
received theme, however trite. Even though poetry
developed to some extent after the foundation of
Islam, in the teeth of opposition from pietist critics,
verbiage had become so extravagant, the formalism
in the handling of hackneyed themes had become
so lush, that all freshness was drained. For many
centuries poetry stagnated in a riot of cliché.

Poetry was no doubt the paramount contribution, perhaps the only art specifically contributed
by the original Muslim Arabs to Islam. The arts in
general merely evolved on the basis of what had
been the various traditions developed in the national territories before they were conquered by

the Muslim Arabs, with some admixtures from India.

Representational art was hampered by the religious prejudice that developed against imitating living beings; a saying was attributed to the Prophet that at Judgment Day the artist would be obliged to bring his creations to life, and if unable to do so would be consigned to hellfire. Though Persians did portray Muslim history and Muhammad's life, and even Muhammad himself, the growth of painting was obviously stunted by this prejudice; sculpture was altogether prohibited.

Hence architecture and the minor arts—notably calligraphy—remained the chief domains of Muslim artists. Decoration replaced representation; all spaces were covered with lush ornamentation. The mosque, an essentially simple structure with an open fountained court and a tower from which to call the believers to prayer, is intricately decorated on every empty space with Quranic verses and the names of Muhammad and the first four Caliphs, generally on enameled tile that gives a soft, subdued atmosphere. Decoration neutralizes the basic austerity of the mosque and at the same time blurs the clarity of the architectural concept.

SETTING THE SCENE FOR MODERN NATIONALISM

Politically speaking, as I have indicated, the Arabs proper soon lost their hold on the empire established by their early élan. The center of the Caliphate was shifted from Damascus, under the Arab House of Umayya, to Baghdad, when the Persians under the House of Abbas took over the destinies of Islam. In their footsteps the first of the many Turkic-speaking groups, who had been organized initially as bodyguards, moved into executive positions and made Islam their own instrument.

It was not to be until the end of the First World War, when the Ottoman Empire transformed itself into the secular modern state of the Turkish Republic, that Persia would change both its dynasty and its state system and the "Arabs" would emerge as a new nationality with ancient roots, much misunderstood.

It may be said, indeed, that the very notion of Arabs as an "ethnic group," in today's terms, remained entirely quiescent for centuries. When the Persians of the "Abbasid" dynasty took over the Caliphate, and then themselves came under the rule of these soldier castes, the Arabic-speaking subjects of the Caliphate as a whole were simply the peasant populations exploited by these foreign soldier castes. The Bedouins themselves, once again locked into the immemorial rhythm of desert life, remained quite remote from the tides now affecting the vast and ramified mercantile society of Islam.

The true "nationalities," so to speak, were the ruling castes, beginning with the Persians and proceeding with the varieties of Turkish rulers that followed. The habit of polygamy made what might be called the biological basis of nationality even more exiguous than in other peoples. It was entirely routine for Muslim lords to have hundreds of wives and countless concubines. Even those who followed the Prophet's recommendation of a limit of four wives—still practiced by the Saudi Arabian dynasty of our own day—found no obstacle in divorcing them at will; though a given lord might limit himself to four wives at a time, he still might have scores or hundreds in the course of a lifetime.

When the Ottoman Turks conquered Anatolia early in the sixteenth century, the Middle East was stabilized for over three hundred years, though most of Islam was cut off from contact with Europe. At the same time, trade shifted from the Mediterranean to the Atlantic, depriving the Muslims of the profits from the carrying trade between India and the West.

This fateful convergence of events marked the massive decline of Islam as a world power. The Arabic-speaking world submitted without protest to the rule of the Turks, which, since they were Orthodox Muslims, also meant the consolidation of orthodoxy. Except for the explosion of primitive reformism associated with the name of Abd al-Wahhab in Arabia in the middle of the eighteenth century, the Arabic-speaking countries remained entirely apathetic politically for many centuries. It was not until the French expedition to Egypt in 1798, under Napoleon, burst open the portals of contemporary Muslim civilization, that the germ of nationalism—to ripen significantly in the next 150 years—was first planted.

In the Ottoman Turkish state the situation from the "national" point of view was still further complicated by the practice, established early on, of staffing the entire state executive below the actual sultan with kidnaped boys, generally Christians, who were converted to Islam and brought up in special schools to assume the administration of the state.

This practice reveals great insight into statecraft. The danger in feudal society was, quite simply, that the throne might be seized by any lord who could summon up a following; hence the landed notables of Ottoman Turkey, by entrusting the fortunes of the state to young men who had no loyalty outside the administration, could counteract the influence of the landed notables themselves and their potentially endless alliances. The so-called slave household of the Ottoman Empire, which ruled for hundreds of years, provided so many advantages for its personnel that Muslim nobles finally began intriguing to secure the juicy positions in the state for their own natural progeny.

For the millennium in which Arabic has been the vernacular of the Middle East and North Africa, the population has been entirely insulated against the nation-state dynamic that began to operate in Europe toward the end of the Middle Ages. Shielded by cosmopolitan Islam and ruled by foreign soldier castes, the masses remained equally insulated against the historical, social, and technical factors that began to shape the modern world a few centuries ago.

It was not, in fact, until the last third of the nineteenth century that European influences, specifically in the form of Protestant and Catholic missionaries, began to act as a leaven on the self-consciousness of the Arabic-speaking Christian communities of the Middle East, especially in Syria, Lebanon, and Iraq.

Though Jews and Christians in Islam are second-class citizens with rights, those rights are severely delimited. Thus the Christian communities engulfed by Islam were allowed to survive, and though subject to various disabilities (such as having to carry on legal activities in the Turkish language), they were not molested in any way. The concentration of Christians remained, indeed, fairly high. Perhaps 10 per cent of the population of the Middle East is Christian—Copts in Egypt; Armenians; Maronites; Melchites; and Greek Orthodox in Syria, Lebanon, and Iraq. These Christian communities were to become the targets for various missionary campaigns in the nineteenth and early twentieth centuries.

The conversion of Muslims has remained a prime target of self-conscious Christians since, no doubt, the first Crusade. In the modern world the problem has, of course, been complicated by the stubbornness of Muslim governments, even weak ones, in refusing to admit any missionaries to Muslim territories if there is any suspicion of a desire to proselytize.

The upshot of this ban on conversion—in any case difficult in Muslim societies because of the violent reaction it provokes (a Muslim is entitled to kill an apostate)—was that Christian missions concentrated on other Christian communities; their activities with respect to Muslims at large consisted of building clinics, hospitals, and schools. Any attempts at proselytization had to be directed at fellow Christians. It became a commonplace in the Middle East for members of the old Christian communities, like the Greek Orthodox and Melchites, to be wooed by American Protestant missions. Whole social or political careers could be based on shifting allegiance from the impoverished, ignorant Greek Orthodox community to the chic Episcopalians and Presbyterians. The question of converting Muslims simply never arose.

It was natural for American, French, and Russian missions to bring to the ancient communities of the

Middle East a more or less "modern" attitude—that is, one that took the national basis of society for granted. Christian communities seeking a bridge to the Muslim majority found it in nationalism and, more particularly, in the exploitation of the one thing they had in common with Muslims—language. The present-day form of the Arabic language was in fact promoted by American missionaries. They modernized printing fonts and launched the large-scale publication of contemporary books, thus flinging open the door of the West to the often irritated gaze of old-fashioned Muslim society. It was thus inevitable for the background of modern Arab nationalism to have been provided by Christians seeking an escape from their communal segregation; the germs of the Arab nationalist movement may be traced to the Catholic and Greek Orthodox communities of Lebanon and Syria at the end of the nineteenth century. Ideas began to stream into the Christian elite, educated in French and much later on in English.

At first the political aspirations of the Christian communities revolved around a number of simple issues. For instance, the Ottoman Government was requested to make some effort to accommodate the sensibilities of its Christian subjects by allowing them to conduct litigation in the local courts in their own Arabic dialect. This demand for local autonomy, aiming at no more than a sanctioning by the Ottoman state of some local concessions, gave rise to a rather modest movement that came to encompass the Arabic-speaking Christian elite of Syria and Lebanon.

At the time nothing more was envisaged; the concept of "nationalism," though it suited the modest political aims of the Christian subjects of the Ottoman Empire, did not imply an extension to Arabic-speakers elsewhere, least of all the densely settled Arabic-speaking Muslim centers in the Middle East and North Africa. At the outset, the movement envisaged no more than the creation of self-governing enclaves in Syria and Lebanon owing allegiance to the Ottoman throne. Many Christians hoped that ultimately, no doubt, states, or at least self-governing provinces, might eventually arise, united by the bond of the Arabic language and consisting, ideally, of local Muslims as well as local Christians.

There was, to be sure, one state already in existence—Egypt—which by the end of the nineteenth century, through the leverage provided by French and British power, had already broken away from the Ottoman Empire. Egypt had been more or less open to European influences ever since its conquest by Napoleon at the beginning of the century.

Egypt already had behind it decades of pseudo-independence—for a long time it had been merely the football of French and British politics—and enjoyed a coherent subsistence as a bona fide state merely subjugated by a stronger state. It was entirely outside the early stirrings of the movement that evolved into a general movement for Arab nationalism. To the extent that the Egyptian elite had crystallized itself out of the descendants of the soldier castes that had ruled Egypt for so long before the advent of the British and French, it began to base itself not at all on the notion of "Arab," still less on the general concept of Islam, but on echoes of the immemorial Egyptian past. For a few generations—indeed, down to our own day—Egyptian self-awareness was anchored in a "Pharaonic" view of itself; its people saw themselves as the heirs of a society rooted in the origins of civilization itself.

Of course, the real connection between the past of ancient Egypt and contemporary Egyptians was so exiguous as to be, for all purposes short of mythology, nonexistent. The Egyptian language had been totally forgotten by the elite as soon as the dynasties descended from Alexander the Great's generals had rooted themselves there. The Greeks had suppressed the ancient religion and wiped out the literature. In this way the elite had been completely split off from the masses of ordinary Egyptians—the most sedentary peasantry in the world, immobilized in the Nile Valley for more than five thousand years. By the time of the Muslim conquests of the seventh century, the Egyptian peasants themselves were ready to give up their ancient Coptic tongue, which expired as a vernacular and was retained by surviving Christians only for the purposes of the Church liturgy. The peasants were speaking ordinary Arabic only a few generations after the conquest. But, as has been noted before, this did not give them any sense of kinship with other Arabic speakers as such, since the hallmark of language as a social criterion came into existence in the Middle East only toward the end of the nineteenth century.

Thus the ancient Christian communities of the Middle East were the first to feel the stirrings of self-consciousness, imposed on them by the clash between the pace of their Europeanization—including the updraft of nationalism—and their *de facto* isolation as Christians in a Muslim sea.

The reaction to European ideas in Muslim communities themselves was infinitely more sluggish.

Though some influential reformers turned up in Egypt around the turn of the century—notably Muhammad Abduh—it would be an exaggeration to make much of a sweeping internal reform of Islam; what impelled Muslims to reform their society internally was not at all the same as what had brought the Christians into the mainstream of Western ideas before them.

Reform in Islam initially had an exclusively material or technical motivation. Beginning, as always, with a desire to heighten the efficiency of the army, the Muslim elite found itself willy-nilly, through its rebellious youth, becoming involved with European culture per se.

This process was far more diffuse than the reaction of the Christian communities to Western civilization. To Muslims, for instance, there was nothing inherently wrong with the Muslim position in the world except for the fact that the world was not yet Muslim, but that had, after all, been accepted ever since the subsidence of Islam in the Middle Ages. In the eyes of Muslim lords, accordingly, the main problem was technical—their armies had to be modernized at all costs to enable them to face European armies.

But of course the key position played by industrial technique in the modern army implied that any modernization was bound to bring about consequences in all other domains of society. Modernization of the army set in motion an immense complex of steps—industrial, organizational, social, and also, naturally, political—that had the blanket effect of swinging the whole society onto a different course. In their ensemble all these steps and measures constituted a shifting of the given "underdeveloped" society into the orbit of European culture.

So it was with the gradual genesis of nationalism in the Middle East. As the Christian communities were touched, first of all, by the ideas coming to them via missionary groups (Catholics, both Roman and Greek Orthodox, and Protestants, generally American), and as they became increasingly dissatisfied with their isolation in Islam, they began dreaming of reshaping society to situate themselves in the "modern" world. Islamic society as a whole also began to undergo the effects of the blanket social upheaval triggered by the reorganization of the army. And, though much more slowly, the Muslim community began to see itself no longer as just the Islamic center of the universe but rather as a nation-state vying with other nation-states in coping with the present.

Thus Islam itself gradually entered the orbit of the West. The technical modernization of Islam's defense institutions was gradually followed by the modernization of society as a whole. In the wake of technology, ideas penetrated the Muslim elite, imported in a complex process of cultural osmosis by the countless individuals who in the wake of army experts and technicians began doing business with the West. Increasing numbers of young people began going abroad for modern education; growing numbers of intellectuals of all kinds began "interpreting" modern ideas for their own still backward readers. Eventually the contagion touched the Muslim aristocracy in the Middle East and North Africa.

The process was, of course, concentrated in the elite; it was also contradictorily articulated. While the elite on the one hand was wholly anchored in its own society—power, position, material interest—and hence in a way the natural guardian of traditional values, it too was bound to respond to the challenge of the West. This tendency was seen, on the one hand, in its perhaps superficial adaptation of current intellectual fashions and, on the other hand, through the natural rebelliousness of its own young people. The pressure for an education abroad, notably in Western Europe and America, was thus reinforced from two different and only slightly convergent directions. Numerically, to be sure, it was only the elite—if this is taken here to mean the rising mercantile strata—that could afford to send its sons (and only a little later even its daughters) abroad to be "finished" in the Western sense. The conservatism of Islam, however, resisted this for a long time—indeed, to this day; nevertheless, even Saudi Arabia, a stronghold of Muslim backwardness, has succumbed to this molecular upheaval.

By the beginning of this century the Middle East was being comprehensively churned up. Nationalism, combined with various notions of political reorganization, such as socialism and Marxism in their various forms, had already established footholds in North Africa and the big cities of the Middle East.

The First World War toppled the Ottoman Empire and flung open the entire area to the play of new forces emanating from the complex of ideas and symbols epitomized by the Soviet Union. Thus the Arabic-speaking countries of the Middle East and North Africa began to assume the shape that is now familiar—a shape that was to become more or less settled as a result of the further reshuffle precipitated by the Second World War.

III

Arabs and Jews: Seeds of the Present Conflict

With the collapse of the Ottoman Empire and the contraction of Turkey into a medium-sized, homogeneous nation-state, Arab nationalism, hitherto limited to modest home-rule schemes in the Fertile Crescent, could contemplate a huge hinterland of people living on contiguous territories—all speaking essentially the same language, and 90 per cent of them professing the same religion. The temptation for idealists inflamed by a "cause" was obvious. The huge area bounded by the Arabic language seemed to be ripe for the simple idea already exemplarily manifest in the countries of Western Europe.

Arab nationalists could expand their horizons well-nigh limitlessly. A far-flung "Arab nation" was grandiloquently speculated about. Philosophy and poetry intermingled. Dreams abounded.

But dreams of unity were to remain dreams for a long time. They remained a preoccupation, very nearly a hobby of the elite. The obstacles in the way of their realization were numerous and formidable.

Yet, by one of those fateful ironies that have proliferated in the Middle East, the crystallization of Arab nationalism was immensely furthered by a new factor—Zionism, the national movement of the Jews. By a curious coincidence, both movements achieved their first formal expression with the carving up of the Ottoman Empire in the immediate aftermath of the First World War.

Zionism articulated in a contemporary political form the ancient longing of Jews that has been expressed in their liturgy ever since their dispersion by the Romans in A.D. 70—the restoration to Palestine, the Jews' historic homeland. Springing up among the Jews of Eastern Europe toward the end of the nineteenth century, as traditional Jewish life was shattered by the impact of modern ideas, Zionism found an effective spokesman in Theodor Herzl, a Viennese journalist and writer, who by the time of his death in 1904 at the age of forty-four had given it political shape.

The Zionist movement had to contend not only with external obstacles but also with the hostility of most Jews, especially those who were well established in Western countries, and those in Eastern Europe, where the bulk of Jews in the world were concentrated, who clung to other "ideologies," such as socialism. Nevertheless, it had made headway in the West, notably in Germany and Great Britain, and as an allied victory shaped up toward the end of the First World War, the Zionist leadership in Great Britain could exercise some influence on the British Government. Many influential Britons were sympathetic to Zionism for either mystical or practical reasons. Some, like Balfour himself, Lloyd George, and others, it seems, were moved by the romantic restoration of the glamorous, mysterious Jews; others, like Winston Churchill, were influenced by the prospect of reinforcing the British anchorage in the Middle East. It may well be, curiously enough, that mysticism predominated (though not a single Arab, to be sure, has ever believed this).

Jewish communities had been sparsely established in Palestine before the First World War, when the region was merely an administrative division of southern Syria. By the end of the war the total population was seven hundred thousand, of which about 10 per cent were Jews.

In 1917 the Zionist leaders were successful in persuading the British Government to sponsor the movement formally. In November the Balfour Declaration was proclaimed, to the effect that the British Government looked with favor on the establishment of a Jewish National Home in Palestine, on the understanding that the interests of the local inhabitants were not to be violated.

The Balfour Declaration was to become entangled in the complications arising out of the dismantling of the Ottoman Empire, an enterprise that soaked up many bureaucratic ambitions on the part of different elements of the British and French governments.

The British had a lengthy tradition of interest in the Middle East: Some of the great monuments of English literature were created by explorers in

Arab lands, notably Sir Richard Burton and Charles Doughty. Indeed, T. E. Lawrence, a British semi-amateur official, came to play a key role; "Lawrence of Arabia" was to become a celebrity. A remarkable mixture of virtuoso, mountebank, and psychopath, with a large head and piercing blue eyes set on the body of a puny eleven-year-old boy, he hypnotized many celebrities such as Churchill and Bernard Shaw by his romantic role. A book describing his adventures—*The Seven Pillars of Wisdom*—was to become a best seller; a popular movie was later made of his life.

Through personal talent buttressed by quantities of gold, Lawrence had secured during the war an alliance of sorts with the sherif of Mecca, Hussein ibn Ali (great-grandfather of King Hussein of Jordan), whose sons, Feisal and Abdallah, agreed to launch a revolt against the Turks with the help of the British. Hussein ibn Ali had lived in Constantinople most of his life; his prestige as Sherif of Mecca (a largely honorific title) was thought very helpful, though he personally was too old and, indeed, too "difficult"—vain, prickly, cranky—to be of much practical help.

The principal tangle, as far as Palestine was concerned, was occasioned by the "McMahon correspondence," an exchange of ten letters between Sir Henry McMahon, high commissioner in Egypt, and Hussein. The letters were written between the autumn of 1915 and January 1916, at the same time the Balfour Declaration was being prepared. Simple in intent, as it might have seemed, the letters did not constitute a treaty between Great Britain and the sherifian family, but "declarations of policy . . . on behalf of" the British Government. The exchange of letters took place not merely while the Balfour Declaration was being incubated, but also during the concluding phases of still another diplomatic operation—the "Sykes-Picot" Agreement, signed on behalf of Great Britain and France by two eminent officials, which split up the Ottoman Empire into zones of influence between Great Britain and France.

The French had long been intimately involved in the Middle East through their long-standing sponsorship of the Christian communities, and now had ambitious schemes of their own; despite the conditions defining their relationship to the British, they were soon to be at loggerheads with them.

The McMahon correspondence stipulated that Great Britain would promote "independence" throughout the whole of the Arabic-speaking world of Asia—for example, the Arabian Peninsula and the Arabic-speaking areas to the north—with the exception of the southeastern corner of Arabia (where Great Britain had special relations with the local rulers) and the coastal strip extending from Damascus northward to Anatolia. At the same time they would undertake not to interfere with French interests. Such "independence" was to arise under a projected British protectorate of some kind.

On the basis of this arrangement and other assurances, an Arab "uprising" was engineered by Lawrence, among others, and headed by Feisal and Abdallah. The operation harassed the Turks in the Hijaz and Syria and aided the successful advance of the British army under General Allenby.

Thus "Arab independence" (within the confines of northern Arabia, Syria-Lebanon-Palestine, and Iraq) in a formal sense was launched.

Though Palestine had not been specifically mentioned in the McMahon correspondence, it might have been thought to be covered somehow by geographical implication. Indeed, Arab spokesmen have often referred to the "twice-promised" land of Palestine as a prime instance of British duplicity.

On the other hand, though it seems that the sherif's family was vexed both by the publication of the Balfour Declaration in 1917–18 and still more by the revelation of the Sykes-Picot Agreement (disclosed by the Bolsheviks in the wake of their *putsch* as an instance of imperialist intrigues), they were soothed without much difficulty. In January 1918, Hussein, now installed as King in Jidda, Arabia, accepted an official explanation of the Balfour Declaration (given by the famous Arabist D. C. Hogarth) that made him "agree enthusiastically, saying he welcomed all Jews to Arab lands." The explanation given to Hussein did not, to be sure, mention the possibility of a Jewish state.

In addition, Feisal, who was supposed to be King of Syria and for a short time actually was, had met the British Zionist leader Chaim Weizmann in June 1918; in the autumn both leaders drew up an agreement. One article endorsed the "encouragement and stimulation" of Jewish immigration and massive settlement on the land, with safeguards for the rights of Arab peasants and tenant farmers; another proposed that the Zionist organization send a commission of experts to be put in the service of the Arab state, and that a survey of economic potential be offered, as well as the assistance that the Arab state needed in exploiting it.

This agreement was signed after Feisal had appeared on the very first day of the Peace Conference in Versailles (January 1919) and expressed his views in a memorandum listing the claims of the "Arabs of Asia." His views on Palestine were very favorable to the Jews; he pointed out that Jews and Arabs were very "close in blood," that there was "no conflict of character," indeed that they were "absolutely at one in principles." At the same time he advocated that the whole area be subject to a protectorate of some big power.

The real conflict at this time was between Great Britain and France, whose wartime alliance had crumbled the moment the war was over. Many members of the British Government felt that their chief enemy was France, even ahead of Bolshevik Russia; the Middle East became a factor in the maelstrom of big-power politics.

A further element was added by the emergence of Abd al-Aziz Ibn Saud, a princeling of central Arabia who had imposed his personal primacy and the primacy of his fundamentalist Muslim sect, the Wahhabis, over almost the whole of the Peninsula, including the Hijaz, reserved by the British for Hussein ibn Ali.

With the Hussein family suddenly excluded from a role in an "independent Arabia," places had to be found for them elsewhere. Feisal, expelled from Syria by the French, was given the throne of Iraq under the British protectorate. Abdallah, who seemed to be squeezed out of consideration by the pressure arising out of the three-cornered conflict among the French, the British, and Ibn Saud, was fobbed off, as it seemed to him, with the governorship of the eastern part of mandatory Palestine between Jordan and the borders of Iraq, Syria, and the Hijaz.

The Palestine British Mandate had originally covered some fifty thousand square miles; the eastern part of this (about four fifths) remained under the British Mandate but was exempt from the provisions of the mandate that had originally authorized collective Jewish immigration.

Ibn Saud's claim to the Hijaz was ultimately accepted, and the situation finally jelled more or less, with the British in control of Iraq and Palestine (including Trans-Jordan); Ibn Saud in control of central and northern Arabia; and the French holding Syria-Lebanon. The Jews were authorized to immigrate into and develop the "Jewish National Home" on an area a little less than 20 per cent of the Mandated territory originally assigned the "Jewish National Home."

The stage was now set for a clash with Zionism. At first, however, the dimensions of such a clash were not at all clear; it was far from obvious that the clash itself would be very serious.

Palestine (the word itself is derived from the Philistines) had never had any "ethnic profile" of its own. Indeed, it had been designated as such by the Romans in order to extinguish its Jewish associations. Arabs themselves considered it merely part of southern Syria. There were not many Zionists among the small minority of Jews living there in 1917, and both Zionist and British leaders thought that the benefits accruing to the largely desolate area by joint British-Jewish development would be welcomed by all. Hence, there seemed to be no profound reason for a fundamental conflict between Zionist Jews and other inhabitants of Palestine.

The larger area that soon came to be the target

of Arab nationalism—that is, all the lands inhabited by speakers of Arabic—was so large (five million square miles) that it might have seemed to dwarf any overconcern with the "tiny notch"—as Balfour had called it—set aside for Jewish immigration.

Yet Arab resistance was to increase steadily. Stemming initially from local irritation with Zionist colonization and with the British Mandate itself, it was to spread to neighboring areas, and eventually, in the wake of the Second World War, come to involve practically the whole of the Arabic-speaking world.

Even in the earliest formal phase of relations between Zionists and Arabs (between the Jewish National Home and the promises to Hussein ibn Ali, Feisal, and Abdallah), there was a marked difference between the interests of the Arab dynasty involved and the enthusiasm of the pan-Arab movement. Though Feisal and his entourage were, of course, Arabs, their specific ambitions were linked to specific areas, like the ambitions of Ibn Saud and other rulers. From that point of view it was easy to accommodate other powers, especially the minute power represented by the Jews in Palestine.

At that time the real shock at a possible discrepancy between a Jewish National Home and the McMahon correspondence or the Sykes-Picot Agreement was felt not so much by the leaders of the "Arab independence" movement (to whom specific promises had been made—that is, to Hussein and his sons) as by the Arab nationalists of Syria-Palestine, for whom the ideal of an "Arab nation" could not be satisfied by a statelet that had to be shared, moreover, with newcomers.

Thus the coincidence of the joint national revival

of Arabs and Jews had far larger implications, even though the collision took place within the small scope of Palestine. To the enthusiastic partisans of Arab unity the colonization of even a small piece of land—especially, perhaps, colonization by a semi-pariah people like the Jews—seemed an outrage against an ideal that encompassed more than the fate of a piece of real estate.

THE RELATION OF ARABS AND JEWS THROUGH HISTORY

This interaction between idea and reality—between the ideal of "Arab unity" and local territorial accommodations—was all the more dynamic because it was played out against the background of the historical interaction between the two peoples. Relations between Arabs and Jews can best be understood against this much broader canvas.

Those relations, densely intertwined under Islam, go back much farther into the past—indeed, as far as immemorial antiquity. "Arabs" enter history—appropriately enough as camel troops—in the service of King Ahab of Israel in 853 B.C.; from the time of the Second Jewish Commonwealth both peoples took their close kinship for granted.

The later books of the Bible, as well as the Talmud and Flavius Josephus, refer to Arabs often. If all the peoples in the Arabian Peninsula who were camel breeders and raiders engaged in foreign trade (especially long-distance trade) are defined as Arabs, the biblical tribes of Ishmael and Midian, for instance, are plainly "Arab" in character. In the stories of Moses, Joseph, and Gideon these tribes are referred to as descendants of Abraham, and thus Israel's direct kin.

Muhammad himself sanctioned this idea officially, so to speak, in the Quran: Accepting Ishmael as ancestor of the Arabs and Ishmael together with Isaac as Abraham's progeny, Muhammad accepted Abraham as the original ancestor of the Arabs. Thus the cousinship of Jews and Arabs was a cliché for both Jews and Muslims.

This had nothing whatever to do with Arabs and Jews being "Semites"—an altogether misleading, biased, and absurd idea. A German theologian, J. G. Eichhorn, at the end of the eighteenth century had assumed, on the basis of contemporary romantic effusions about the link between ethnic identity and language, that those who spoke Semitic languages— of which Hebrew and Arabic are the best known— were also related by "race." The notion was simultaneously complex and obscure, and all the more meaningless in respect to the various peoples, remarkably variegated both culturally and physically, who spoke Semitic languages. The notion of a "Semitic" race or people has bedeviled discussion to this day; a huge body of scholarship was to spring up buttressed by later theories about the ancient Hebrews having been just one more "Bedouin" tribe originating in Arabia. It has in fact become almost a banality that the ancient Hebrews were Bedouins.

Yet it is obvious that the whole emphasis on Israel's wanderings in the desert, as recorded in the Bible, is that this nomadship was most *unusual*. It was explicitly described as an ordeal for the ancient Hebrews just because they weren't accustomed to it; it was seen merely as a brief interruption of their real life as a farming people. This interval between their lengthy sojourn in Egypt and their settlement or resettlement in the land of Canaan, where they plainly lived an ordinary rural life as farmers and herdsmen of small animals—sheep, cattle, goats—must be distinguished from the dromedary-centered existence that characterized true Bedouin life. There is a substantial difference between pastoralists wandering within a settled area and those dependent on the camel in the great reaches of the desert. The Bible never says that the Israelites were camel breeders or nomads, or that they ever came out of Arabia at all.

If a definitive proof is needed from literature, it should be obvious that the entire Bible is redolent of the atmosphere of a farming and shepherding folk inhabiting its own tilled land, whereas Arabic literature, especially poetry, is steeped in the desert life, rotating around camel breeding, of the original Arabs. This is all the more striking because the romantic literary tradition of the desert came to be cultivated with passionate intensity by entirely sedentary people generations after the initial Arab eruption from the Arabian Peninsula.

The notion of the Twelve Tribes, often taken to reflect tribal life in the desert, is merely a misconception; tribalism is not confined to Bedouins, or for that matter to nomads in general. (Witness the tribalism seeming to underlie even the densely cultivated Yemen of thousands of years ago.)

Yet disregarding any notion of a "Semitic" race, the kinship between the Hebrews and the camel-breeding businessmen of Arabia must have been real enough. The remarkable influence exercised by both Judaism and Islam can be explained, in fact,

only by the one feature common to ancient Hebrews and to desert Bedouin alike: democracy.

In sharp contrast to the great societies of Mesopotamia, Egypt, and Asia Minor—especially those
that flowered in Byzantium and Sassanid Persia—
both ancient Israel and the Arabian Bedouins were
characterized by a basically classless society, an absence of compulsory obedience to a central authority, freedom of speech, and an egalitarian attitude
toward the individual. Despite the authority invested
in individuals as rulers, both cultures felt that
people were, simply, equal.

Underlying the notion, essential to monotheism,
of the total sonship to God inherent in the idea of
the One God was this primitive democracy, which
may, perhaps, even have facilitated the development of monotheism to begin with. When Gideon
pointed out that the Lord, and not he, was to rule
over Israel, he was expressing the paramount feature of Hebrew monotheism in a form that has run
through the history of Israel down to the present.
Similarly, in the first few generations of Islam,
when the executive was still Bedouin, the Caliphate
was entirely democratic.

Privileged classes existed, to be sure, but the
differentiation between them and the rest of the
population was not calcified by the legal system (as
for instance in the celebrated and generally speaking progressive Code of Hammurabi). The very
law that is often taken to be a hallmark of backwardness, the "eye for an eye" notion, indicates
that in the eyes of the law all people were the same.

A similar conception of slavery was also common
to the two peoples. A slave was not considered to
be a mere chattel or beast of burden, as he had been

in industrial societies (in the Roman Empire, for instance, as well as in the United States and in the Russian Empire until the nineteenth century), but rather a member of the owner's household entitled to as much respect and affection as anyone else, and sometimes with even more independence. An excellent example of this is in Genesis 15:3: Abraham's servant, Eliezer, called "the son of the house," is entitled to inherit the property if a natural heir is not found. The humane, natural, and intimate treatment of slaves in ancient Israel is reflected in the classical Hebrew Prophets, who while castigating Israel quite hysterically for countless transgressions, never refer to any ill treatment of slaves. Ancient Arab sources, as well as accounts written by great explorers like Doughty, bear out the existence of the same relationship in Arabia.

The role of women too in both ancient societies showed similarities. While not participating directly in public discussions, women were thought to have a special "power" mystically inherent in their being. In ancient Arabia they were celebrated not only as authors of poems like dirges and paeans of praise, but also for their satirical expertise. The scorn of women poets was regarded as a weapon so powerful that it might actually turn the tide of battle. Just as Saul was supposed to be terribly chagrined when "dancing women" sneered at him for having killed ten times fewer people than David, and Baraq would not attack Sisera unless Deborah went along with him (in the Book of Judges), so Muhammad is recorded, against his usual practice of reconciliation, as having had two women satirists executed. To this day Jewish women from Yemen —the oldest and most characteristically Jewish community in the world, and the most characteristically Arab part of the Muslim realm—compose poems of all kinds, mainly satirical, about public events.

Since Israel was never truly nomadic, in sharp contrast with the Bedouins of northern and central Arabia, it would be foolish, no doubt, to attribute these pervasive resemblances to a mere socio-economic similarity. The Bible itself is doubtless near the mark in recording an original kinship.

Each people, naturally, had   ections of its ancestors. The Old Testament i   tly a collection of the sagas and legends revolving around the distant and near ancestors of the Hebrews. Though lacking substantial written records, the Arabs also had some memories of both their ancestors proper and kindred "Arabs who had vanished," remembering various ancient Arabic-speaking peoples who had appeared on the periphery of much higher cultures (Syria, Iraq, Yemen) and had been assimilated by them. One people who had played an important role, for instance, were the Nabateans, the immediate eastern neighbor of the Jews during the crucial centuries that spanned the Jewish revolt against Rome, the smashing of the Jews as a settled people, and the emergence of Christianity. The Nabateans, who had abandoned Arabic for the great language of the eastern Middle East, Aramaic, had been intimately involved with the Jews, both positively and negatively.

Abraham is recorded as the father not merely of Israel and Ishmael, but also of many tribes from northern Arabia and for that matter from Sheba, doubtless an echo of an original connection with the ancient country of Sheba in southern Arabia.

He is reputed to have sent those sons of his away from Canaan, which he had reserved for Israel (Isaac) alone.

The feeling of kinship between Israel and various tribes in Arabia might have come about because, whatever the causes of an original "Abrahamic" exodus from Mesopotamia to Palestine, some segments found Palestine too crowded. The group epitomized in the names of Lot and Esau (Edom) left for the tillable regions east and south of Palestine, while the Ishmael-Midian tribes turned off along the great trade routes leading east and south into the Arabian Peninsula from Beersheba. Along this enormous trek they no doubt mingled with other peoples, and gradually became the mélange of businessmen and brigands characteristic of all Bedouin tribes (whose existence was anchored in the domestication of the dromedary camel presumably toward the end of the second millennium B.C.). It was this dual phenomenon—the trek from Mesopotamia and the deflection of a big section into Arabia, along with the domestication of the dromedary—that was to create a special society later to be welded together by the Arabic language.

Most important, no doubt, about this indubitable affinity based on kinship and an early common history was the egalitarian stance peculiar to both peoples, which gave them an entirely disproportionate impact on mankind.

It is curious that the national histories of both peoples originate with the formation of religions that shape and define them: the Jews under Moses, the Arabs under Muhammad. An overwhelming fact about the destinies of both is that in both cases the national history was put into a form that could somehow be assimilated by entirely different peoples.

Both the Old Testament and the Quran (and for that matter the New Testament too) are completely parochial in character. The Old Testament very plainly records nothing but the specific history of Israel; the Quran has an even narrower compass. Yet both have become, without seeming contradiction, paradigms for the imagination and ideas of countless other peoples, who have simply grafted their own interests onto the corpuses evolved by Israel and the ancient Arabs. The Old Testament is the foundation for a third of mankind, the Quran is the same for another sixth; both together, accordingly, constitute the spiritual groundwork of half the world.

Though it is true that other religions such as Buddhism have spread far and wide, these have always been based on more philosophical conceptions of the universe that could easily be accepted and digested by other people. In the spread of Christianity and Islam, however—both engendered in different ways by the original impulse of Jewish monotheism—this phenomenon is made altogether unique by virtue of the parochial nature of the transmitted material. It was not *merely* an idea that was taken over, but an actual history book—an account of events that had taken place elsewhere among totally different people. Because the explanation of those events could be taken as having universal significance based on the idea of the One God, the history book itself could become sacred.

This could be only, no doubt, because of the underlying notion of democracy common to both. Once God is elevated beyond the world and is conceived of as the unique repository of all authority, all social stratification is trivialized; the individual human being is brought into a direct relationship to the true source of Being. Hence both Israel and the ancient Arabs, while in the very midst of making a parochial record of their national experiences, gave them a universal form.

CULTURAL DIVERGENCES

It is just this common kinship that also highlights the profound differences that were to characterize the histories of Jews and Arabs. The key factor here is surely timing—the great gap that separated the formation of Israel from that of its Arab kin.

There was, after all, a jump of more than two millennia between the genesis of Judaism and that of Islam. Moreover, the Jews had taken more than a millennium, approximately twelve hundred years, to shape the religion and consolidate it; Islam was established in three generations' time. A further differentiating factor was surely the total contrast between Judaism and the environment it evolved in (though it was, of course, greatly influenced by the complex civilizations under whose tutelage it grew up, notably Egypt and Babylonia).

Israel developed its uniqueness at a time when it was a small and relatively helpless people, in sharp contrast with the overwhelmingly hostile environment to which it ultimately succumbed. By the time of Muhammad, Judaism was already an established model. In addition, the Arabs had had a common consciousness for more than fifteen hundred years; the Bedouin and their offshoots occupied not only the whole Arabian Peninsula, but also had drifted into southern Persia, Iraq, Syria, and Egypt. To be sure, most of the Bedouin who had infiltrated the more advanced civilizations had been absorbed, yet those remaining in considerable numbers in Arabia—the commercial transfer point for the Persians and the Romans (who for seven centuries had constantly been at each other's throats) —could benefit by their neutrality.

Perhaps more important, from the point of view of the internal evolution of the Arabic-speaking peoples, was the disintegration of the highly civilized ancient kingdoms in southern Arabia that for a variety of reasons had collapsed just before Muhammad. These highly developed societies then merged with the rest of the Arabic-speaking tribes of central and northern Arabia. This was vital for the spread of Islam as well as for its inner development. The numbers of the Arab tribes were substantially increased at a time when the ancient societies of the South, incapable of being organized on a national basis, could not develop sufficiently separate identities to become different nations—as had surrounded Israel so many centuries before.

Though the scattered tribes of the Arabian Peninsula spoke mutually unintelligible dialects, they were all united, somehow, in the possession of a literary language, used both for poetry and for business between tribes. To be sure, the tribes had their own petty gods and local cults, but those pagan cults had not undergone any particular elaboration; no priesthoods had been evolved; the holy shrines were few and far between and at the service of many tribes.

By the time of Muhammad, the combination of these factors had produced a situation in which a relatively small spark could fuse the whole of the peninsular population into a single force, creating almost overnight a single religion professed by a single nation. In contrast with the somewhat ramshackle structures of Byzantium and Sassanid Persia, the Arabian tribes under Muhammad's leadership, carrying the message of Moses, could become the most powerful single element in the Middle East.

This was quite different from the fate of Israel. Israel was one of the numerous petty kingdoms of Syria and Palestine that, while all speaking essentially the same dialect, had nevertheless evolved into autonomous states reposing on highly organized clergies. Israel emerged, in short, at a time when it was too small to hold its own, or rather the other way around, when its neighbors were too well developed to be influenced very much by Israel's religion. The Jews had found themselves stifled, as a petty kingdom among others; the universal message proclaimed by the Hebrew Prophets could not have a dramatic effect on the small peoples surrounding them.

Arab cosmopolitanism also constituted a profound difference. The chief business of the Arabian tribes—long-distance import and export—required countless Bedouins to be entirely at home in foreign civilizations. Muhammad himself, born into a thriving town that lived on the caravan trade, as well as his companions, the future rulers of the primitive Muslim state, were heavily engaged in the far-ranging business network constituted by the brisk trade between the Romans and the Persians passing by southern Arabia. Before their role as conquerors in Syria, Egypt, and Mesopotamia, the

Bedouin had previously infiltrated all these areas as traders; their expertise in handling clients proved to be a priceless preparation for their later activities as rulers and administrators.

In contrast, when Israel had developed, the overwhelming bulk of Jews had been farmers with no training—unlike salesmen—in accommodating the point of view of outsiders. Combined with their unique religion, cast in a form practically incomprehensible to their pagan neighbors, this self-absorbed, parochial attitude tended to make them intransigent, demanding, and difficult—altogether lacking in the urbanity characteristic of traders.

The agricultural past of the Jews was reflected in their schedule of festivals and holidays: The day of rest, one of the most influential ideas in history, and the month of rest were calculated to give all farmers respite from their labors. Muhammad was quite familiar with the notion of the Sabbath, but completely disregarded its aspect of repose; instead, he singled out an entirely subsidiary, though ceremonially impressive idea—that of assembly and prayer. Muhammad's Arabs had no use for a day of rest, since the Bedouin never did any regular work at all; the merchants would have been seriously inconvenienced by a regular weekly break in their long-distance transport enterprises. Thus on the basis of what would seem to be purely practical considerations, Islam never accepted the religiously grounded notion of the Sabbath as a day of rest.

In law, too, there was a sharp contrast between the Jewish and Arab attitudes. For farmers all possessions are important; hence all transfers are safeguarded by a complex network of laws and customs. Every type of transfer of property is characterized by special circumstances that preclude the formation of even the idea of "contract." (This accounts for the immense ramifications of detail in the lengthy discussions embedded in the Talmud; the word for contract is nonexistent in ancient Hebrew.)

Traders, on the other hand, are bound to evolve abstract categories for handling large numbers of commodities for a general public. Individual objects are reduced to the general—they become merchandise pure and simple. Thus the idea of a contract, which handles relationships and categories, becomes imperative.

There is an even more striking difference between the family attitudes of ancient Jews and Arabs. In the realm of inheritance, for instance, it is natural for farmers to wish to keep their property undivided; hence the law of most agricultural peoples, including the Jews, is based on primogeniture: The first son inherits the whole estate; the others get mere compensation. The daughters do not inherit the land together with their brothers, but are married; in the absence of sons, a daughter may inherit the whole estate, on the assumption that a husband will surely be found for her.

Muslim law, on the other hand, generally splits up estates into small shares, so that only cash or camels could be divided conveniently. Even an only daughter never inherits more than half an estate. Doubtless anchored in the allocation of booty in tribal warfare, this notion of inheritance, though not very suitable for settled populations, is still in effect in most Muslim societies.

Thus, for farmers the natural social unit is inevitably the family—father, mother, or mothers, children, servants, and laborers hired by the season. For the nomads, the tribe or clan is the unit required by the need for organization and self-defense in its rovings about.

The Jews throughout history have been characterized by a feeling for intense family life. The family among the ancient Hebrews was the simple one now known as the "nuclear" family—the house or the farm run by the father. This is reflected at the very beginning of Jewish self-consciousness in the simple, moving accounts of the Old Testament. This simpleminded attitude has been diffused throughout the world, indeed, by the Bible.

This is sharply contrasted with the Arab view, though life as it was to develop among the sedentary Arabic-speaking populations of the Islamic East was assuredly a far cry from pastoralism. Nevertheless, the ancient attitudes of the far-ranging nomads have persisted to this day. In the primordial societies of the Arabian Peninsula, which have lately been much publicized by the staggering increase in oil revenue, the image that comes to mind as a reflection of the national ethos is not the intimate family circle but the huge reception hall. This remains the characteristic feature of eastern houses, thronged by a crowd of people related to each other by countless degrees of cousinship, uncleship, and so on. What counts here, and still counts in Saudi Arabia and Yemen, is the *clan*, of which every member is proud to be a part.

There is another antithesis between Israel and the ancient Arabs that must explain many aspects of the rapid diffusion of Islam. I have mentioned the primacy of the Arabic language, whose remarkable expansion was without doubt the most fundamental change brought about by the spread of Islam. The original contribution of the Arabs under Muhammad was, indeed, just this language. The inspired vehicle of Moses' message to the Arabs in their own tongue, the "noble Arabic Quran," was the essence and for that matter very nearly the sole content of what the Bedouins brought out of Arabia. Singularly rich and capable of protean change as well as sonorous and altogether beautiful in the ears of its speakers, Arabic could become a vehicle of civilization almost instantaneously.

Because of their virtual fanaticism about language, the Muslim Arabs took it as a matter of course that *their* religion had to be conveyed in *their* language, which was imposed in consequence on peoples from the western coast of Africa to the borders of India.

Apart from the countless practical reasons for the spread of Arabic, this one cardinal element—the sincere devotion of the Arabian nomads to their own language—must have been the key to their insistence that the Holy Quran be read only in Arabic. History has rewarded them richly for this devotion, though to be sure they have paid a heavy price throughout the ages in other ways, since the reverence paid the sacred idiom instantly led to a sort of hidebound formalism. This was evident from the earliest times and was given a concrete expression, for instance, in the holding up of pre-Islamic models of poetry as the paradigm for literary art in general. A premium was put on abstractness, artificiality, and ornament at the expense of feeling and originality. This artificially maintained separation between poetry and life, encased within an unbending and entirely arid traditionalism, may

have been a chief cause, as it was a chief consequence, of the stagnation that still burdens Arabic-
speaking society to this day.

The Jews, on the other hand, however devoted
they were to their sacred scriptures, never clung to
their language in any sense. They changed languages as they moved from one place to another,
secure in their identity no matter what language
they spoke. They never thought to prohibit the
translation of their scriptures into whatever language came to hand.

The remarkable wealth of the Bible, itself a tiny
fragment of what must have been the original productivity of the ancient Hebrews, is very striking.
In addition to its unmistakable art—much of it,
after all, unsurpassed—what is more evident is its
liveliness, its intermingling of real situations and
people that even after three thousand years gives it
a singular vitality.

If Arabic poetry, precisely because of its richness
and complexity, sometimes gives the impression of
being purely ornamental, Hebrew poetry seems to
convey the essence of genuine feeling.

One of the numerous paradoxes in the relationship between the two peoples may well be that
Hebrew poetry was so intensely alive, so concentrated in its expression of feeling about real values,
that it never found imitators, even among later
Jews. Arabic versification, on the contrary, could
easily be imitated just because it was so artificial
and complicated, and was imitated throughout Islam
even in those areas where Arabic itself was not
spoken. The crowning paradox was no doubt the
experience of the Jews in the Middle Ages, in Spain
and elsewhere in Arabic-speaking Islam, when He-

brew poetry was itself remodeled along the lines of the dominant Arabic.

Thus in our own day, when language is practically the overriding hallmark of ethnic identity (overlooking such exceptions as Switzerland), the *de facto* presence of Arabic as a vernacular throughout North Africa and the Middle East has brought about the abrupt transformation of the Arabs into one of the numerically impressive peoples of the modern world—despite the countless divisions among them of class, politics, geography, and economics.

RECIPROCAL RELATIONS OF ARABS AND JEWS

There is a curious ambivalence in the intertwined destinies of Arabs and Jews since the emergence of Islam.

Under Islam the great and ancient peoples of the Middle East lost their identities—that is, their biological descendants became Arabic-speaking Muslims. This was chiefly because farmers suffered inordinately under the mercantile civilization of Islam. But while the Jews, who before Islam had been farmers, manual laborers, and artisans for centuries, ceased being farmers, they managed to survive in their new roles as traders, artisans, and professionals.

This profound transformation was brought about by what has been called the "bourgeois revolution" of the ninth century, which turned the Middle East into a mercantile, industrial, and bureaucratic society—at a time when Western Europe was still at bottom a farming community ruled by feudal nobles and knights. From the tenth to the thirteenth centuries especially, Islam gave Judaism a different shape. Arabic itself became the chief language of the Jews, who used it for everything but the liturgy, while the handling of Hebrew was greatly influenced by Arabic philology.

Thus it may be said that while the Jews were the ultimate source of Muhammad's religious inspiration—which launched the Arabs as a united people on a career of world conquest—it was the Islamic society founded by the Arabs that gave the Jews a socio-economic profile they retain to this day.

This process of transformation was itself worked out on the foundation of Muslim principle. Though in theory Islam is a militant religion—grounded in the necessity for perpetual war until the entire world has been converted—it has always had another aspect as well. Throughout his career Muhammad always clung somehow to his original belief that he was doing no more than expounding the same simple truth he had inherited from his illustrious spiritual forebears—Abraham, Isaac, Jacob, and Jesus. The Quran, in fact, expressed both tendencies. Thus the holders of one attitude or the other could always find scriptural support for their views, and the policy might differ in accordance with the shifting circumstances of a given Muslim society.

By and large, Islam in its orthodox versions (the bulk of Islamic society at all times, especially the Ottoman Turks) was always singularly tolerant. In fact, it was only certain sectarian Muslims who developed the fanaticism that came to be attributed by Christendom to the Muslim world as a whole. These were notably the Almohads (Muwahhidun="Unifiers," of the One God), members of a ferocious movement that conquered North Africa and Spain in the twelfth century. They invaded some of the most prosperous Jewish communities established there and simply slaughtered those who refused to accept Islam. Life was made difficult for the enforced converts too, since of course the fanatics were quite well aware that a forced conversion could hardly be sincere. They imposed a severe surveillance on them, made them dress in a special way, and considered them more or less as outlaws. The converts were often tried and executed on flimsy or nonexistent grounds, and their wives, children, and property were turned over to Muslims. In a word, all the excesses of the Spanish Inquisition were anticipated by the Almohads.

There were, to be sure, notable exceptions among even sectarian Muslims, such as the Fatimids, who ruled Egypt and Palestine in the early Middle Ages (969–1171). Though Shiite sectarians with Berber support, these were the most liberal rulers of the Middle Ages. (In our own day it may be of interest to observe that most of the sectarian Muslim movements that persecuted non-Muslims have also been non-Arab.)

In fact, Muslim attitudes toward non-Muslims varied substantially from era to era and from country to country. It is probably fair to say that by and large the position of non-Muslims under Arab Islam was far superior to that of the Jews in medieval Christendom—largely because of a cardinal difference between the attitudes of Islam and of Christianity to outsiders. The Roman Catholic Church simply denied the right of other religions to exist; Islam accepted it. Of course, the non-Muslim groups in Arabic-speaking countries were far more substantial and powerful than the defenseless Jewish settlements in medieval Europe.

Toward the end of the Middle Ages the status of non-Muslims under Islam deteriorated sharply. The ruling castes of foreign barbarian soldiers regarded the local populations as cattle to be exploited ruthlessly. Their rapacity became particularly oppressive around A.D. 1300; by reaction, the more the native Muslims were oppressed, the more fanatical they themselves became vis-à-vis religious minorities.

But with the consolidation of the Ottoman Empire in the fifteenth and sixteenth centuries, tolerance was restored once again; the Turkish sultans of the sixteenth century especially were celebrated for it. It was not, indeed, until the central state in its turn declined that non-Muslims began being treated harshly once again, together with the local population itself. Nevertheless, despite all the vicissitudes, the general principle underlying Islam—the right of other monotheisms to exist—was generally followed.

Before the general decline of Islam parallel to the rise of Western Europe at the end of the Middle Ages, the Jews who settled in Arabic-speaking countries had constituted the majority of world Jewry. Later, however, the Jews who settled in Christendom became more influential; they were to participate in the dynamism displayed by Western Europe from the end of the Middle Ages on. The Jews who remained in Arabic-speaking countries—none at all in central and northern Arabia—were now an insignificant fraction of Jewry as a whole.

When Zionism was introduced into the Middle East in a practical form in the 1920s, the balance was shifted once again. Now basically a European people, the Jews have re-created a small state in the heart of the Middle East—at the very moment that a new wave of self-consciousness is sweeping through the Middle East and indeed through Islam as a whole. The paradox of this situation is easily summed up: At the very moment that the East itself has been stirred by its collision with the West into the promise of new life, it finds the natural focus of its renewed energies epitomized by a feeling of hostility to the West. Hence since it is inevitably regarded as a European outpost by the awakening national consciousness of the Arabic-speaking countries, Israel is a natural target for hostility, all the more so in view of the traditional role of the Jews in Islam as helpless pariahs. Thus the Jews, the oldest living people, now beginning as it were from scratch in the State of Israel, are having the greatest difficulty persuading their neighbors and the world at large to accept them as a state-wielding people.

IV

Decay and Growth: The Arabs Today

The turmoil of the twentieth century, crystallizing in the upheaval of the First World War and its aftermath, has shaken up the ancient communities of the Middle East and North Africa. It has given them new life, new forms, new institutions. The world at large has become aware of an old society reborn.

The contrast I have mentioned between the old and the new is the first thing that strikes an outsider in the Arab world today. In the big cities, fleets of motor cars surge back and forth; trucks, high-powered luxury cars, and jalopies shuttle among oil fields, palaces, slums, fields, and across the deserts. Outside the towns, in Africa and Arabia proper, the wilderness stretches out in varying degrees of aridity. In the Fertile Crescent, meadows and farmlands, lavishly watered, present a startling contrast to the desert profile elsewhere.

Bedouin stride along the spacious thoroughfares looking at skyscrapers where people live like those on Fifth Avenue, Avenue Foch, or Belgravia; the cafes are filled with Europeans, Arabs dressed like Europeans, and sheiks in their desert robes, gold bands holding silken kerchiefs around their heads.

The change has spread far enough to encompass women, too. In Cairo and Baghdad, to say nothing of Algiers and Rabat, women will be found walking about as self-sufficient and chic as their sisters elsewhere, many without veils. Even the women who still wear them will often seem as emancipated as their unveiled sisters, merely clinging to the veil as a vestige of old-fashioned decorum.

Yet looming up beyond the human contrasts, the stage set, so to speak, creates an ambiance of sameness that stretches from one end of the Arab world to the other. If the populations are motley, the atmosphere is remarkably homogeneous. The general look of Muslim towns is unmistakable; every community bears witness to the fundamental changes laid down by Islam long ago.

THE EVOLUTION OF THE MUSLIM TOWN

The big cities of the Middle East are surely the oldest inhabited places in the world. Damascus has been inhabited without interruption for more than five thousand years; Jericho in Israel must be nine thousand years old. If it is true that the city is a prerequisite for civilization as such, the role of the ancient civilizations of the Middle East in this respect, too, was decisive.

Though Islam began as a religion taken up by

nomads and extended far and wide by their conquests, town-building was the foundation of the
new society. Muslim notions of a town revolved
around its suitability for a focal principle—the interaction of religious duties and social ideas. While
the obligatory communal prayer, for instance, was
held in the open air with no limit on the number of
participants, the Friday noon service, the cardinal
prayer-time, was held only in a fixed settlement
with a permanent population with at least forty
legally responsible adult men present. Later on, the
Friday service had to be carried out under a roof in
a totally enclosed mosque.

This alone indicated the degree to which Islam
was conceived of as an urban religion; nomads
plainly could not accomplish all this. Muhammad
himself, who had grown up in the biggest town in
contemporary Arabia, had at the very outset cast
Islam in a mold designed to suit businessmen, high-
lighting the values of sedentary life based on agriculture and commerce. The conquests that
launched the Muslim empire were guided by the
town leaders of Mecca and Medina; the Bedouin
merely provided the manpower. Nor did the Bedouin way of life—far-flung wanderings determined by the needs of the camel—play any role in
the new social scheme. The Bedouin and their immediate descendants soon settled down. This was a
natural consequence of the subsidence of the primacy of kinship in favor of faith—it was fundamentally the townsmen who were favored.

Just as cities were vital for antique society and,
no doubt, for civilization itself in the nature of
things, so in Islam cities were the matrix of life.

They were, in fact, the only places where the right life as laid down by Islam could be lived. Thus when the Bedouin occupied far-flung territories, it was natural for them to be wary of living as a small minority in highly developed urban areas thronged with non-Arabs; they had to create towns from scratch. The new towns took on the form of armed encampments set up to control the countryside, sometimes close to an older urban center (such as old Cairo), and fairly isolated from rival settlements (like Kufa in Iraq, or Qayrawan in Tunisia). Such towns would symbolize the power that had been able to set them up; Baghdad became the spiritual focus of the Abbasid dynasty as well as its political center. Such created towns would be the result of planning, in contrast with the "spontaneous" development of many centers that simply sprang up around a sanctuary, the tomb of a saint, and so on.

Long before the Muslim conquests, the gridiron arrangement of the old Hellenistic towns had been functionally contradicted, as it were, by the growth of individual quarters. The Muslims consummated this process. What had begun long before them as the more or less random infiltration of outlanders was rounded off by the systematic reshaping of urban customs in accordance with the new ideas generated by early Islam.

In its broad outlines, the classical ideal of an integrated city still survives, by virtue of the centrality of the mosque (which replaced the forum, or agora), as well as by virtue of the walled enclosure of a general area composed in terms of the discarded classical gridwork, still discernible in countless towns throughout the Arab world.

What gradually smothered the gridwork was the

overriding notion of religious allegiance, reflected spatially in town quarters based on the contrary ideas of seclusion and secrecy—indeed, downright segregation. This feeling of seclusiveness has been commonplace throughout Islamic history: The most sensible attitude toward the government was aloofness at best, hostility at worst.

A full-fledged Muslim town contains two foci: the mosque and the market. The mosque, the spiritual focus, is generally placed on the main avenue, if possible where it crosses the other main avenue. Next to it generally stands the chief edifice of the government, either the ruler's palace or the residence of his deputy. Thus the mosque is both the political and religious center of the town. The crowds congregate there to hear the proclamations of the government: the mood of the congregation may play an important role—even negatively, through violence, if no one turns up at all. It is from the mosque that the preacher would recite a blessing every Friday on the ruler, thus acknowledging the ruler's legitimacy. The omission of such a ceremony would be a blow struck at the ruler. The mosque is also the spiritual focus of a Muslim town, since the learned leaders of the community congregate there regularly for discussions and teaching.

As for the markets, they too are always much the same in Muslim towns. Those who deal in the same kind of wares always occupy stalls next to each other, and whole market lanes are reserved for single trades. In addition, the hierarchical layout is likely to be the same everywhere: The religious aspect of the mosque is served by dealers in candles, incense, and perfumes; the intellectual aspect by booksellers and bookbinders, with leather merchants and the slippermakers next to them.

Then come the textile merchants' halls, the only ones generally featuring a roof. These can be locked so that valuable goods as well as fabrics can be warehoused and sold. The textile halls have evolved no doubt from the Byzantine basilika (probably the market halls of Antioch served as models). Throughout the Middle Ages textiles were the fundamental industry, much like the metal industry of our own day, and the textile halls served as international warehouses for the trade with both Christendom and the Far East.

Next to the textile dealers are the carpenters, locksmiths, and coppersmiths; a little farther toward the outer edges are the smithies. The outer limits of the town reserve their greater spaces for the industries that need either the actual space or some remoteness because of a nuisance element, such as the dyers and tanners. Outside the town limits will be the potters. The city gates will serve as backdrops for fairs; if caravans are important for the town fair, there will be a space for them to be assembled and unloaded. Outside the walls there will be the singers and storytellers surrounded by crowds of passersby.

In settling their new towns, the first Muslim Arabs arranged themselves by tribes; each tribal quarter had to have its own mosque, bath, and generally its own market. In Baghdad, from the very outset, Persians and Arabs lived apart. In Tlemsen, separation between the natives and the descendants of the old Turkish janissaries is very much alive to this day.

Indeed, many Middle Eastern towns and cities

are still composed of mutually exclusive, interlock-
ing ghettoes, all illustrating the same ancient principle of town-building. In contemporary Antioch,
for instance, as well as in Damascus and Aleppo, the
cities are in no sense unitary, but are constituted by
villages made up of communities that are not only
separate but also hostile. Each community lives independently of the others; to this day intermarriage
between villages that have been living next to each
other for centuries seems out of the question. In
Antioch an Alawite would not dream of going into
a Muslim mosque, and until recently an Alawite
sheik would never have risked going into town on
the day of public prayer for fear of being stoned.
Any public demonstration carried out in any one of
the communities is bound to be taken as a sort of
challenge to the others; the fear of massacre—very
nearly commonplace throughout the Middle East—
arises naturally out of the segregation and its attendant suspicions and hysterias. In a milieu whose
instability encompasses such dangers, ordinary people's desire to live as secret a life as possible becomes entirely understandable. Since each community is virtually self-sufficient, the city consists of
some forty-five tiny quarters, like so many autonomous cells or cities within the city, each with
its own civil head, religious leader, council of
elders, and even police, represented by night
watchmen.

Within all these quarters there is hardly any
piazza or square to compensate for the narrowness
of the alleys. A well-to-do Muslim house is situated
so that it turns away from the street, getting its
light from an inner patio—a custom inherited by
Spain and passed on, oddly enough, to suburban

buildings in California. The ideal is maximum privacy. The general desire for privacy is heightened by the tradition of secluding females; windows and roofs are built so as to maintain a maximum of secrecy in day-to-day living. Similarly, the doors on opposite sides of a street are not supposed to be opposite each other.

The minorities, of course, also have their own quarters. Until recently Jews would live next to the government center for the sake of security, but the tensions arising out of the war with Israel during the past quarter century have altered this pattern. Most Arab countries have expelled the overwhelming bulk of their Jews, except for Morocco; those remaining are in need of constant protection, which they may sometimes get from the government.

The initial allegiances of the individual in the Arabic-speaking world are first to his family, then to the quarter he lives in. People live in a particular quarter, indeed, because of kinship, either of blood or of faith. Inhabitants of different quarters may of course meet in the market and the mosque. Minorities have their own stalls in the market close to the corresponding business section held by the Muslims, but there will generally be a traditional allocation of crafts to one group or another; they are not shared.

The atmosphere of seclusion arising out of the compartmentalization of space in Muslim towns is reflected, very naturally, in all social life. It is very difficult among contemporary Muslims to know an individual's true opinion about anything important. This is commonplace, to be sure, perhaps everywhere; but in modern Islam the conformism is more deeply anchored. There is unquestionably a big chasm between public protestations and private belief. Because of the dense interaction in Islam between social ethos as a whole and religiosity it does not even help to know that many young Arabs today do not go to the mosque as much as they are supposed to. Regardless of their prayer schedules, these same young Arabs, for instance, may well be among the most fanatical partisans of Islam. This is no doubt a consequence of the role played by religion in the national consciousness of so many Muslims; since religion has been the chief contribution of the Arabs in the past, it is felt by many young people to be dangerous as well as deeply distressing to abandon it. Hence it may well be praised in a sort of political sense by those in whose inner lives it has no meaning whatsoever.

To this day, in fact, appearances play a preponderant role in Arab manners; social life is permeated by a meticulous etiquette. Courtesy is the hallmark of behavior, regardless of what may be going on underneath. It is much the same as the prevalent handling of language—floweriness, ornamentation, and high-flown rhetoric are far more highly valued than content.

This contributes to another celebrated syndrome associated with Arabs—hospitality. This is surely a fact, especially among the Bedouin, where the well-nigh biblical tradition of ardent receptivity to outsiders is still a matter of course.

In the desert, where there is no central authority, and every cluster of people is responsible only to itself, the importance of hospitality is obvious; its absence would mean, quite simply, mortal peril for the unprotected stranger. For this reason, no doubt, hospitality involves an exaggerated graciousness intended to show the stranger that he is *not* in peril; he is made to feel for the moment like a son of the house, afforded the protection of the tribe as long as he remains there, and indeed afterward. The "breaking of bread" is a sort of umbrella guarantee, if it is given at all, that the stranger is the beneficiary of the tribe's good will.

This echo of the desert has overflowed into ordinary life today; Arab hospitality, the legend of the desert, is taken seriously everywhere. In a way, of course, it is rather like the old-fashioned legendary attitude toward wayfarers held in medieval Christendom as well—indeed, held everywhere in the world before the industrial age.

The emphasis on hospitality may underlie what is, perhaps, the most outstanding of Arab personal traits—a kind of charm, commonplace among the Bedouin and the cultivated classes, and present even among the somewhat reserved and suspicious peasantry. Arab behavior constitutes the very essence of charm—a bland, unaggressive, and affable penetration of the stranger's desires, so that he feels he has been anticipated by the Arab's eager, unforced willingness to please. Coupled with intelligence and energy, the impact can be overwhelming. Sometimes, to be sure, when applied in large doses outside normal intercourse, as in political discussions, it leads to a sort of bewilderment on the part of the outsider because it is spasmodically interrupted by the intrusion of its opposite.

Countless Westerners have been entirely disconcerted to see a previously amicable and optimistic political discussion suddenly dissolve into an emotional, "fanatical" harangue, accompanied by their Arab hosts' wild predictions of general doom.

After a balanced presentation of a more or less factual situation, the Arab intellectual—cultivated, charming, appealing—suddenly seems to put on a different mask—or, of course, take one off!—when a political nerve is hit.

It is, no doubt, an aspect of the tension that keeps surfacing in modern Arab life—the tension of the conflict between reality and an ideal. By being superimposed on facts, the ideal situation that is longed for provokes an outburst of emotion.

This in turn may reflect the radical ambivalence I have pointed out in the Arabs' attitude toward the West. On the one hand, it demonstrates an unequivocal assimilation of everything in the West without exception—from technology to music to poetry; on the other, a frenetic desire to reject the whole thing and to reassert their own heightened, energized personality. Thus the personality of many Arabs tacks defensively back and forth between the forces of change and those of tradition.

THE LEGACY OF THE BEDOUIN PAST

It is the deserts that have preserved the primordial, truly "Arab" way of life—that of the camel-breeding Bedouins. But what are these nomads like, after all? The nomadic way of life is so strange to the bulk of mankind—nomads today cannot constitute more than a tiny fraction of 1 per cent of the world's population—that most people fall back on sentimental literary stereotypes that portray the Bedouin as either a sort of desert knight sweeping fair maidens off into the desert or a furtive villain stalking about on a motheaten camel. Yet nomadism had persisted in Central Asia, the Arabian Desert, and North Africa for millennia.

The essence of tribal life is that the individual is encased within the universe of the tribe. This means, of course, that inwardly the Bedouin accepts only the authority of the tribe; vis-à-vis strangers he has an attitude of tranquil equality regardless of who they may be.

Psychologically, nomadism may be summed up as independence. The look of a Bedouin entering a city for the first time is unmistakable. He may own nothing but the rags he is standing barefoot in, but as he strides along the avenue, past the shops, buildings, and factories, all the monuments of civilized life, he is, plainly, profoundly unimpressed. It is simply the way outsiders are living—entirely meaningless to him.

The atmosphere of nomadic life is altogether different from that of the peasantry. By nature the Bedouin is accustomed to dealing with all sorts of different people, from his own vantage point of urbane detachment. The Bedouin has a sort of humorous indulgence for the toiling and moiling of peasants and businessmen, living as they must in tiny houses, rooted to the ground, doing the same thing day after day, and unable to enjoy the free wind and indolent life of the desert—where the women, of course, do all the work and the men sit about discussing the situation.

It may well be that the fabulous wealth of the Arabic language—its cultivation as a poetic idiom and its status as the most precious possession of the Bedouin—came about through just this habit of endless chatting, the chief pastime of the desert. The Bedouin are naturally eloquent—they are used

to conversation and have all the verbal sophistication of Parisians. They have, indeed, excellent
salon manners. Love of poetry, a trait of the ancient Arabs of the desert, well attested by the accumulation of pre-Islamic poetry, has survived in the
modern Bedouin.

The free life of the desert may be responsible for
what had been commonly noted as the absence of
any race feelings among Muslims. Many Bedouin
nowadays are blacks, no doubt the descendants of
former slaves, and have been for many generations.
Arab traders played a disproportionately large role
in the slave trade, which not only still exists in
Muslim countries but indeed has been intensified
with the recent influx of oil money. In any case, it
is plain from the behavior of Bedouin toward each
other, both black and white, that there is not the
smallest trace of racial feeling.

The atmosphere of two friendly Bedouin tribes
at a joint feast, for instance, highlights the absence
of feeling precisely because of the jocular style in
which manifest racial differences are referred to.
Though most white Bedouin are spare in build,
with snubby features quite unlike the "Semitic"
stereotype, there are also Bedouin, especially
around the Fertile Crescent, who reflect the Semitic
image—aquiline noses, high cheekbones, full lips,
and strong beards. If such a tribe, for instance, finds
itself lolling about under the tents over a feast of
mutton, much badinage will go on between the
"Jewish-looking" and the "negroid" ones—the first
sneering gently at the sparseness of the blacks'
beards and their sooty color, and the blacks roaring
indulgently over the heavy beards of the others,
their hooked noses, and so on.

The symbiosis between the nomad and the camel is curiously close. Utterly dependent on its legendary capacity for doing without water—it is the only animal that can sustain long sojourns in an arid wilderness—the Bedouins seem to have a love-hate relationship with the camel, incontestably one of the most annoying of animals.

Huge to begin with—much bigger than a horse—and peculiarly irritable, the only way a camel can be persuaded to do anything is by systematic growling, grunting, hissing, gargling, and barking. Baby camels, to be sure, are completely winning—tiny, in proportion to the size of an adult, they can be picked up and carried in one's arms. But of course the Bedouin do not regard them as pets—camels are simply indispensable.

Horses, on the other hand, inspire affection similar to that felt by Westerners for house pets. Though horses are useful only in special situations, they are such ornaments, as well as status symbols, that it is common to see them being pampered.

Bedouin life has been eroded to some extent by the course of evolution. In the modern periods, with the density of communications intensified, and with the pressure of the state growing heavier and heavier, the Bedouin too have fallen into the web of social relations. The late King of Saudi Arabia, Ibn Saud, began experimenting in the twenties with settling the Bedouins. He had some success; if the Arabian Desert is ever irrigated, the Bedouin will no doubt find themselves turned into farmers by way of exploiting their predilection for animal husbandry, a natural transition to a settled life.

Politically speaking, it may be a paradox that the Bedouin, no doubt the "purest" Arabs, are the least interested in Arab nationalism, as they are also, of course, utterly indifferent to the cluster of modern ideas that have ravaged the modern world—the various abstractions of democracy, socialism, communism, and Marxism. Sublimely nonintellectual, while at the same time highly intelligent, they have seldom, except for eccentric individuals, shown the smallest interest in the nationalism of which they might easily be considered the very epitome. Perhaps this parallels the indifference of blond, blue-eyed Scandinavians for the extravagances of "Nordic" theorizing among the Nazis.

From the point of view of a Bedouin, the notion of his being linked to a peasant or city-bred "egghead" by virtue of their speaking the same language has something grotesque about it—in fact, a Bedouin regards the speech of the land-bound peasants as a debasement of his own noble tongue.

Indeed, since Bedouin regard *all* interference with their way of life as vexatious, they generally consider the Israelis no worse than the other city-based governments that meddle with their freedom. For that matter, the Israelis, who have made a systematic effort to settle their own Bedouin via the transition to animal husbandry, have shown great consideration for them, and have been rewarded by a substantial degree of allegiance. The Bedouin were far less sympathetic to the Muslim Turks.

It may be that the rhythm of desert life is inherently unique. There is a tranquillity about being oriented toward the vastness of nature, a vastness, moreover, uncomplicated by disharmonies of detail. All seems unchanging—the endless desert stretching before one, the camel striding rhythmically along for hours, the soft chanting and singing, the desultory conversation; the life of the encampment, the "black tents," the bustle, the children milling about, the women preparing food, the men gossiping endlessly about any topic that comes to mind, from affairs of state to the scandals of Hollywood.

To the extent that the Bedouin become settled, they naturally become farmers; as the property structure is integrated with surrounding society, some of the notables become wealthy, and thus tend to merge with their counterparts in settled society. After all, the present Saudi dynasty, consisting of thousands of princes, originated only a couple of generations ago as minor chieftains—and now they have all that oil!

The Bedouin do not count for much numerically; there are only a few million in the Arabic-speaking world, though since they have the run of the steppelands, they are spread over an immense area.

The great Arab magnates are, of course, the one element of the population that has made its mark with particular force on the awareness of outsiders. The combination of the magnates' bearing, their high morale, the seemingly romantic conditions of their way of life, and now, above all, the sudden influx of well-nigh boundless wealth, has deeply impressed the imaginations of Western observers.

The tribal feeling of an organic independence that characterizes the manners and attitudes of the great Bedouin tribes is also reflected in the Arab lords, who are generally connected in some way with the great tribes, at least in their self-awareness, rooted in the very beginnings of Islam itself. Just as even an ordinary tribesman is encased in a self-assurance derived from his being totally aware of just who he is, so is the Arab Muslim notable deeply sure of constituting in the very nature of things the apex of the world's aristocrats.

This is especially so for Muslim Arabs because, in addition to being the exponents of the last and therefore the definitive religion of mankind, they are genetically, so to speak, connected as Arabs with the very inception of Islam, which began, after all, as the handiwork of one Arab and is expressed, to boot, in the noble language they are all proud of. Thus a Muslim Arab lord has the cozy feeling that the universal religion his forefathers bequeathed to the world is somehow or other his private possession.

When the British encountered the great lords of the desert, for instance, they were immediately aware that "native" or not, the lords were masters of men by nature and despite their material inferiority could deal with the British on a footing of equality. Even the illiterate Bedouin who came up against the Colonial Office representatives of Great Britain at the end of the nineteenth century were not impressed by anything the British brought with them but their guns. When the late King Ibn Saud, founder of the Saudi Arabian dynasty that has been cutting such a swath in the global economy in the past few years, heard his longtime adviser, St. John Philby (father of the celebrated Soviet spy), explaining that he was undecided about how to get to San Francisco from Arabia—whether by going east or west—it did not embarrass the King in the least to show his astonishment that Philby could manage it one way just as well as the other. The King merely inquired, looked dubious, was reassured that the world was, indeed, round, laughed, and went on. Similarly, when the King, hearing Philby talk about a conversation he had had with some Americans, asked him how that was possible, and Philby, slightly puzzled, said they talked the same language, the King was not at all put out at learning that the Americans were not, as he had thought, all red Indians.

WOMEN AND POLYGAMY

Perhaps the single element in the life of the Arab lords that has most fascinated the West has been their sexual lives. Everyone knows, of course, that polygamy exists. Yet the notion of polygamy on such a large scale as found in the Middle East and North Africa, among living people whom one may actually meet and talk to, still has something stupefying about it.

In the press reports touching on the oil crisis of 1973 and 1974, for instance, there were many references to the King's half brother "so and so," or "so and so"; a rough estimate was sometimes made describing the family as consisting of a "clan" of several hundred princes. But it was rare to see the situation accurately assessed.

Yet it was quite well known that the old King Ibn Saud, who followed the rigorous practice of having only four wives at any one time, nevertheless had managed, by changing wives entirely legally—indeed, piously—to leave behind well over 700 or 800 children (more than 350 sons were acknowledged; female children were not publicly registered).

Clearly the dimensions of the institution take a special effort to grasp. When it is recalled that many Muslims do not limit themselves to four wives at a given time and in addition may have limitless numbers of concubines, all of whose children will be legitimate, it is obvious that the contrast I have mentioned above between the patriarchal "nuclear" Jewish family, and the clan family traditional in Islam, is heightened to a staggering degree in the case of affluent Arab lords. Westerners cannot really imagine what family life means when a man is linked in marriage to hundreds of people; the household consists, essentially, of the women's households where the children are brought up and where the husband is a visitor. The fact that the institution has subsisted to our own day, upheld by people otherwise urbane and cultivated, remains, no doubt, a puzzle.

In the same way, Arabs' love relations seem strange to Westerners. Obviously women are not treated anonymously; preferences remain paramount. A man with hundreds of wives and/or concubines will prefer some to others. (Ibn Saud was famous for being madly in love with one of his numerous wives.) Nevertheless, the puzzle remains: What can the relation *be* between the husband and what may be called the rank-and-file of the harem?

It is obvious, of course, that the gargantuan development of the harem system implies nothing in particular about actual sexual activity, except in the negative sense; it tells us, perhaps, that the women are not having much of a sexual life, except for the well-authenticated prevalence of lesbianism (notorious in the great harems of the Ottoman Empire). The notion of enforced sequestration implied by the very word "harem" seems to give one a baffling glimpse into mysterious mini-universes.

Muhammad himself was, no doubt, displaying either a singular personal disposition or mere sexual chauvinism in ordaining the limit of four wives on the assumption that four wives could be adequately taken care of—four wives, indeed!—but when that relatively modest figure is multiplied by factors of ten, what on earth is one to think of what really goes on? For all practical purposes, evidently, nothing; indeed, the very multiplicity of wives may make it possible for a shy husband to lead a quite torpid sexual existence; his "image" cannot be damaged, since it can always be assumed that he is lurking about in someone else's bed—the larger the harem the vaguer the location.

Thus, though it is a matter of pure routine for Arab males to make much of their machismo, there is no reason to accept it at face value—to be taken in by pretensions that are at bottom no more than an etiquette of stereotyped symbolism.

By restricting the children to the mother's surroundings, the harem system may normalize them beyond the neuroses that in the West have been surfacing for so long, perhaps partially through the attractive explanations found by Freud and others. Thus children will have the mother's loving care—since Arab women are as loving as healthy women everywhere—while looking up to the father as a distant model who does not have time to interfere too much. In early childhood, at least, if the child's chief guardian is a loving woman, the foundations would seem to be well laid for the older child to express his attenuated relationship to his father via some form of political emulation.

Whether or not this is characteristically the case, however, there can be no doubt that even the rugged simplicity of the desert, on the other hand, has produced its own generation of neurotics and misfits; the well-publicized behavior of some of the Saudi princes, for instance, yields nothing in extravagance to better known Western models of disorder.

This, too, is changing, of course, if only because the women of the Middle East are getting an education very nearly as rapidly as men. Even in the vastnesses of Saudi Arabia, the stronghold of conservatism, it is impossible to keep people from learning about the outside world. When a Saudi Arabian prince makes a state visit to Western Europe and takes along his favorite clutch of wives and children, those wives do not, after all, molder in their hotel rooms—they go out shopping. And no matter how many intermediaries, interpreters, and servants they have interposed between themselves and their surroundings, they see everything—especially the way other, Western women behave.

It is no doubt women who will batter down the iron gates of traditionalism. Their relationship to the outside world is bound to be more practical. A lord going abroad on business really lives in much the imperial manner he does at home, giving orders to servants and amusing himself with entertainment, girls, and so on. A woman, however primitive, who goes abroad for the first time and sees the accumulation of commodities openly displayed becomes in her own milieu a sort of time bomb. The shopping sprees of Arab ladies with limitless funds that have become notorious in the past couple of years bear within them, as Marx might say, the seeds of future dissolution.

For the time being, however, the numerous educated women throughout the Arab world are emotionally insecure and still feel the deep conflict between the public and private spheres of life. A Saudi woman whose husband takes her and their children to London because it is the *right thing* to have his family near him, then surrounds himself with other women in some other flat and has her visit him to watch his carryings-on, may put up with it—what else can she do? But she may weep when alone, and—more important—confide to an Englishwoman, for instance, that when her sons grow up they will not be like *him*—the father. She no longer accepts her servitude inwardly.

Even though there has been a vigorous—indeed, vociferous—women's movement in the Middle East for more than half a century, the traditional forces within Muslim society are still very much in control. Despite the legislation to liberate women socially and legally, marriage customs persist. The ancient custom of arranging marriages by heads of families is still widespread, even in Egypt, and in cities. Child marriages, too, are still common, even though these are explicitly forbidden by legislation. Marriages can still be arranged by a simple contract, independently of registration with the authorities. A father's decision is all-powerful: A girl who is threatened by her father with repudiation of her mother, deprivation of future financing, or outright expulsion from the house, is very likely to abandon any projects of her own.

The family remains the center of traditionalism, making the contrast between its own framework and the freedom of the big world outside, in which a woman can, indeed, rise to prominence—in medicine, the law, government, or business—a natural source of inner turmoil.

Perhaps the source of the whole syndrome remains the simple fact that in Arab society a man's decision is basic. A man can repudiate a woman without specific reasons; a divorce will be effective on the spot. The woman has no such privilege; she may, indeed, *sue* for divorce, but the proceedings can be interminable if her suit arouses her husband's opposition, while he, of course, can remarry whenever he feels like it.

Thus even though Islam at the very outset did a good deal to ameliorate women's dependence on men—by restricting the number of wives, for instance, to merely four!—and even though many apologists for Islam defend it with respect to its treatment of women, it can hardly be denied that the burden of Islamic tradition has generally been, in spite of partial reforms, rather antifeminist to this day.

The old-fashioned acceptance of male supremacy —"male chauvinist piggery"—is sharply contrasted with another, equally old tradition that complements it. In the Fertile Crescent and to some extent throughout North Africa, homosexual friendships are considered entirely natural, even commonplace. Friendship and erotic love between men is not merely tolerated, but is regarded as the zenith of cultivation. Though this acceptance of homosexuality seems to be inherited from both ancient Persia and Greece, and is commonplace both in Persia (outside the orbit of the Arabs) and in Egypt, it is found throughout the eastern Mediterranean and North Africa.

Thus, whenever Arabs come in contact with outsiders, and especially since the establishment of Israel in 1948 with Westernized Jews, there is a natural barrier to communication. It is only too easy, especially for Europeans whose own attitude tends to be healthily parochial, to regard various aspects of Arab behavior as in and for themselves "perverse." On the Arab side this is complicated by a tendency to look on the free-and-easy relations between the sexes in Western society as entirely contemptible.

This is, to be sure, changing rapidly, like so many other aspects of the Arab world; it may even be that a large portion of the somewhat hysterical behavior of the urban masses in the Middle East and North Africa arises out of the deep malaise generated by the uprooting of old habits in response to the demands of modernity, and in the course of change will eventually taper off.

VILLAGE LIFE

Numerically the preponderant element among the Arabs today is what has always been preponderant throughout human history—the people of the land.

The essence of peasant life is its sameness, or rather, its dependence on the rhythm of the seasons. In Syria, Lebanon, Egypt, Iraq, and throughout North Africa, the life of the fields remains what it had been for so many millennia—devoted toil within the bosom of a natural environment that while varying from one extremity of the Arab world to the other is generally manageable. For countless generations people have scratched out a living from the poorer parts—with the help of a goat!—and prospered in the richer parts.

The goat has played, in fact, a quite disproportionate role in the life of the Middle East. Though many people think that the goat created the Sahara Desert—superimposing on the general process of desiccation, which must have begun millennia ago, its own type of nibbling (which is to snatch up the entire tussock by the roots)—the goat was essential to farmers and pastoralists because of its remarkable ability to find sustenance anywhere while producing a huge amount of rich milk.

In most ways an individual's true universe in the Middle East is the village. Villagers are reserved, suspicious of strangers, low-key, wrapped in a humdrum routine enlivened by seasonal changes and their own animal vitality. Village life has always been connected, of course, with the life outside—if only by the needs of commerce and barter—but it is only very recently, with the advent of radio and television, that illiterate villagers have been brought into contact with the big centers. That aspect of life has been changing very rapidly, though village life still remains essentially what it has been for many centuries.

There are villages in the Middle East within a stone's throw of each other in which the inhabitants, for countless reasons—generally religious— have never intermarried, and the villages have preserved their identities as villages since time immemorial. Identical in language and largely in customs, the villagers of one village regard others as strangers, and hostile strangers at that. This is largely the effect of the invasions that took place more than thirteen hundred years ago. When Islam assumed dominion over this huge area and eventually governed it, countless little pockets remained, especially in the hill country, that held out against the mass tide of conversion. It is like the segregation of quarters in a Muslim town, writ large. The Maronites of Lebanon, for instance, held out more or less *en bloc*, clinging to Mount Maron and managing to withstand the advantageous tug of conversion. Since there was no actual compulsion at any time, such holdouts were never coerced; they gradually established the patchwork still in existence, especially in Lebanon and Syria.

Even the rise of secularism in the Fertile Crescent has had little effect on the age-old life of the villages, remote from the mainstream of "ideology" and still wrapped up in their own routine. As elsewhere, to be sure, young men leave their villages for the big towns and even abroad, so that the real intellectual life of the country is carried on in the towns. At the same time, the villages really constitute the core of the national psyche.

They are intertwined, of course, with the "middle classes" of the towns; the bourgeoisie, indeed, is recruited from the energetic, entrepreneurial elements of the villages. And it is the middle classes that provide not only the bulk of the individual leaders but also the infrastructure of all government. Though Islam has long since followed in the footsteps of Western business, and the Muslim bourgeoisie is engaged in all levels of international commerce, still the role of businessmen in Islam proper has progressed at a slower rate than that of the entrepreneurs in the Christian communities.

LEBANON: CROSS-ROAD TO THE WEST

It is only natural, no doubt, for the Lebanese, the descendants of the ancient Phoenicians, to have played an exceptional role in business life. For generations Lebanon was a financial center for the whole of the Muslim and Arabic-speaking Middle East. With the consolidation of oil wealth, more particularly, Beirut became a rendezvous of the newly rich lords of Arabia because of its marvelous climate and nearby mountains and accessibility.

Recent events in connection with the current tension in the Middle East—the civil war of 1975–76 in Lebanon that may not have come to an end even now—have suspended the role of Lebanon in international affairs; its fate is now linked more than ever before to the settlement of the feverish hostility that has pervaded the Middle East since the confrontation of the United States and the Soviet Union in the Middle East and the establishment of Israel in 1948.

Still, Lebanese Christians have survived both in Lebanon and abroad. Their cosmopolitanism is rooted in their international connections: It would surely be ridiculous to look for exoticism in Lebanese businessmen. Without risking an overgeneralization, it is safe to say that beneath their cosmopolitanism they are in all respects like any group of Western businessmen.

A half million Lebanese Christians have been American for generations. The Arabic names now popping up in American politics generally belong to the children of such formerly Arabic-speaking Christians; in coming to America they were simply getting away from the Turks and the Muslim world in general, for which the word "Arab" was no more than a synonym to them. There is a community of similar size in South America, and a disproportionately influential though smaller and more scattered community of Lebanese or Syrian businessmen throughout West Africa.

With long-standing anchorages in France, England, and America, the Lebanese Christian community that made up almost half of Lebanon finds it natural to wear European clothes, to speak French and/or English, and to feel genuinely at home in the West just in an era when their homeland has finally been engulfed by large-scale, pervasive Westernization. Lebanese women follow the fashions avidly and gossip about celebrities and social intrigues just like women in Europe and America. Lebanese men buy boats and houses, go in for business coups, visit nightclubs, and live in fact indistinguishably from their counterparts in France, England, and the United States. They are generally called a "bridge" to the East but actually serve to highlight the cultural homogenization now taking place on a cosmic scale.

It is a curious grace note to the flux of politics that just at a time when Arabic-speaking Christians were fleeing Islam by immigration to the New World, their kinfolk in Syria and Lebanon were trying to accommodate their Arabic-speaking Muslim milieu by launching a version of "Arab" nationalism that would enable them to break out of their parochial seclusion. Subsequently the children and grandchildren of the first wave of Arabic-speaking Christian immigrants nevertheless often thought of themselves as "Arab" in order to fit in with ideas in

America, where one's "roots" are generally linked to the country of origin. Now, in our own generation, with Lebanon well-nigh stifled as an expression of Christendom, and with Muslim Syrians—with a socialist bias, to boot—at the helm, the Syro-Lebanese in America are having second thoughts. As the religious element, thought to be outmoded, has nevertheless surfaced again in the Middle East, and as the word "Arab" is beginning to resume a more obviously Muslim connotation, the psychological stance of many young, practically assimilated young Syro-Lebanese in America is becoming ambivalent.

The fate of the Lebanese Christians, both in Lebanon and abroad, will no doubt be settled as part of the general process of integrating the Middle East, Muslim and Christian, with world affairs. The involvement in world trade that was typical of the Christian role in the Middle East in the nineteenth century was itself a process essentially identical with the overriding activities of Islamic civilization in its glorious past. Once the Muslim community began recovering from the stagnation of the past few centuries and made its entry—or re-entry—onto the world scene, the specific role of Arabic-speaking Christians was bound to be overtaken and no doubt absorbed by Muslims. The fate of Christians as such in the Middle East will ultimately depend on the extent to which the resurgence of Islam will foster enough secularism to enable minorities to live in harmony with the majority.

NEW PLAYBOYS

The recent oil publicity has beamed a glaring light on the highjinks of Arab notables and their ladies abroad. In some respects the publicity seems merely banal—it is rather like the stories about *nouveau riche* Americans at the turn of the nineteenth century, before the great American fortunes had had time to be taken for granted.

The buying up of houses for astronomical sums, the indulging of fantastic whims, the wholesale purchase of entire inventories of anything at all, the gambling of extravagant sums on the turn of a wheel—all these seem instances of conventional ostentation.

It has become routine for rich Arabs to pour into the great capitals of Europe. There is an interaction between available funds and politics; Europe has become especially popular because of the heat in the Middle East, both literal and metaphorical.

In London and other capitals they swing about nightclubs and casinos and take advantage of the medical care that is so much better than what they can get at home. Shopping, too, is the only thing to do in a strange city if there is enough money available; it is also the greatest fun. In London hundreds of millions of dollars are spent on tourism alone. It has been calculated that the average Middle Eastern visitor—an average that includes, of course, secretaries as well as sheiks—spends twice as much as the average American, hitherto the top spender.

The buying up of houses and flats, used both for business—a prime motive for travel—and for vacationing, has made quite a dent on the real-estate situation in London, since the houses are bought on the top level, a third of a million dollars and up.

One well-known house in Belgravia—the chic section of London—was sold to a sultan for $1 million; a six-bedroom flat was sold for $600,000.

Crown Prince Fahd, Deputy Prime Minister of Saudi Arabia, is reported to own three houses in Belgravia. A businessman, Muhammad Mahdi al-Tajir, the ambassador to London of the United Arab Emirates, bought a castle an hour and a half away from London for $1.2 million—an indoor swimming pool, an indoor tennis court, more than a dozen bedrooms, elaborately painted walls and ceilings, an underground tunnel to its west pavilion, and more than 800 acres. The ambassador also bought a Scottish castle.

A prince from Abu Dhabi—one of the notable back alleys of the world—rented a suite at a good London hotel for about $1,700 a day for himself and his entourage. Ten per cent of the clients at a famous London gambling casino were Arabs; the manager reported seeing one of them lose more than $400,000. The shopping sprees at famous luxury shops, like Harrod's, concentrate on fur coats and bathtubs. A jeweler in New Bond Street reports having "several hundred sheiks" as customers; he gave a conventional explanation: The sheiks, he said, like to put "pretty things" on their women. No doubt the women had a say in the matter. The same jeweler has opened outlets, moreover, in Oman, Abu Dhabi, and Qatar, with two more coming up in Kuwait and Bahrain, respectively.

The Saville Row tailors have had considerable success in outfitting not only notables but also their staffs; those settling down to long-term relations with Britain have as it seems given up their traditional clothing; they are content with imitating the well-dressed Englishman.

Curiously enough, at the very moment that vast material resources have been superimposed on a lengthy tradition of lordliness, as exemplified in the great princes of Arabia, individual members of now incredibly affluent families seem to be making a public display of what can only be called vulgar snobbery.

The Saudi playboys thronging London nowadays, for instance, have acquired a reputation for fantastic vulgarity on all levels; they behave like traditional social climbers. Longing to be seen with the "right people," they have fallen for the usual phonies, deadbeats, and spongers that all capitals teem with. Having on arrival begun their social careers by hanging about with tarts, they swiftly graduate to supertarts—bogus Italian countesses and down-at-the-heels English gentry.

At the same time, amid the general lavishness of display, the Arab lords have shown a curious independence of spirit. Many high-level merchants, such as art dealers, had expected the Arab lords to splurge on art, much like the Japanese tycoons who began making their mark on international life in the wake of the Second World War. Art dealers sat about expectantly, waiting for Arab *nouveaux riches* to build up huge collections on the advice of knowledgeable insiders. Great schemes were concocted for conning the newcomers.

But it soon became apparent that whatever luxuries the lords were going in for, picture-buying was not one of them. Whether or not the indifference of the Arab notables to the charms of the plastic arts is to be linked to the celebrated prohibition, based on Muhammad's misunderstanding of the Mosaic interdiction of the creation of images, the parvenu plutocrats have shown no interest whatever in any form of art.

When money began to splash about them they simply reinforced their interest in what they were already interested in—high-speed motorcars, perhaps now gold-plated, from which they could shoot, with equally high-powered rifles, the increasingly rare Arabian gazelle; air-conditioned palaces in the desert; gambling, and house-buying—all the normal bustle of large-scale acquisition. Since they had not liked art and since, to boot, they don't care whether they *should* like art, they simply don't buy any.

The Middle East, in short, has taken its normal place in the world. Its leaders have donned their present authority with an inborn matter-of-factness; the lordliness peculiar to Islam's conception of itself, reflected in the morale of its notables, invests them with an easy composure.

In sum, Islam, which at the outset established an unprecedentedly ramified mercantile society and was then submerged by the rising West, has once again plunged into the mainstream of international exchanges. Islam cannot find this distasteful; along with its spiritual interests, it was always worldly. Indeed, in our own day we see the society established a thousand years ago fulfilling itself as it failed to do, so to speak, because of previous historical diversions—the Mongol invasions, the desiccation of the deserts, the discovery of the New World, and the encirclement by the industrial West.

The exploitation of the oil resources has merely restored the balance—a little convulsively, to be sure, but in accordance with the movement of the epoch.

V

The New Ferment

At the outset of the Second World War the elite throughout the Arabic-speaking world was being worked over by contending ideas. Socialism and nationalism, in their varying aspects and versions, were in the air.

Fascism, including nazism, had made some inroads in the Fertile Crescent, though not very seriously. The converts made by socialism were mainly among the Christian communities, though in North Africa socialist ideas were commonplace. For a long time Muslim society as a whole remained impervious to large-scale ideas of world reform.

The former territories carved out of the Ottoman Empire, though still short of independence, had taken on a new shape. Egypt was autonomous; Saudi Arabia was, practically speaking, independent. The French still seemed securely anchored in Syria, Lebanon, Tunisia, Algeria, and Morocco; the Italians seemed brilliantly successful in Ethiopia and Libya.

In Palestine the British had bogged down in political difficulties. The Mandate, established in 1920 on fifty thousand square miles on both sides of the Jordan and ratified by the League of Nations, was soon modified as far as the Jewish National Home was concerned: Trans-Jordan, the eastern portion —about four fifths—of the mandated area, was insulated in 1922 against collective Jewish settlement. Though inhabitants of Palestine on both sides of the Jordan were properly known as "Palestinians," it became easy to think of Trans-Jordan as distinct from western Palestine.

Jews were settling in the country, a little sparsely, reclaiming the desert areas, increasing productivity, and establishing institutions.

Though divided by religion (Muslim versus Christian, Christian sects versus each other) and as yet untouched by the "ideology" of Pan-Arabism, the Arabic-speaking inhabitants of Palestine during the thirties were giving the Zionist leadership and the British more and more trouble. By the time the Second World War broke out, the Arabic-speaking inhabitants of all Palestine—and indeed of the whole Middle East—were downright hostile to the British or at best neutral; the Jews were willing to fight the Nazis together with the British wherever they could.

Just before the Second World War, accordingly, the Arabic-speaking world, most of it still subject to foreign powers, was on the brink of independence, though the claims put forward by the champions of "Pan-Arabism" would still have seemed extravagant.

To be sure, the fermentation of politics did not affect life beneath the surface. Only the elites of the various countries still divided from each other were each affected in different ways by current fashions—nazism, socialism, and communism (the last only as a trace element—the Soviet regime was in no position to expand). A diffuse current of Pan-Arab propaganda emanating from the countries of the Fertile Crescent had to contend with the religiously tinged apathy of the Muslims, the parochial apathy of the Christians, and the poverty of the illiterate masses in general.

Economically the Middle East and North Africa were remarkably depressed, except for Palestine and the parts of North Africa administered by the French. Poverty was endemic everywhere; illiteracy was almost as widespread, except in Palestine and Lebanon. Disease, too, was rampant, especially in Egypt, again with the exception of French North Africa and Palestine.

Yet even before the Second World War, as we have seen, a new factor had made its appearance: oil. Discovered long before in the Persian Gulf in quantities important enough to attract European attention, it had taken some time to be properly assessed. By the eve of the Second World War, King Ibn Saud, anxious to buttress himself to some extent against the British, on whom he still largely depended, gave a concession to some American oil interests to look for oil; it was found shortly before the outbreak of the war. It was still not quite clear how abundant it was, but by the end of the war it became obvious that the whole of the Persian Gulf was, practically speaking, floating on a sea of oil—Persia, Saudi Arabia, Kuwait, Bahrain.

It was a factor that was to have the most momentous consequences. Indeed, the titanic events set in train by the Second World War, along with the discovery of oil, were to transform the Arab world.

The British withdrawal from India and the shattering of the French Empire entailed drastic changes in the status quo throughout the Middle East. Syria, Iraq, and Lebanon emerged as independent states. The independence of Saudi Arabia, secure in the possession of oil resources that were soon to prove formidable, was consummated. The British in Egypt, while seemingly still in control, were hard pressed by the sprouting of an indigenous movement on purely "pharaonic"—non-Arab—lines. In Libya the collapse of fascist Italy had been followed by Libyan independence. And southern Arabia, Yemen, and the petty sheikdoms around the Gulf of Oman, though seemingly calm, were soon to be drawn into a maelstrom. In North Africa, which still gave an impression of stability as a French overseas holding, the independence movements that had been simmering for decades began to acquire a cutting edge.

And in Palestine the British mandate was about to collapse, opening the way to the establishment of two successor states—Israel and the Hashemite Kingdom of Jordan.

THE ROLE OF THE INTELLIGENTSIA

Perhaps the paramount element in the complex of forces that has been remolding the modern world since the First World War has been the intelligentsia, which in the Middle East and North Africa has played the same disproportionately thrustful role as it has in all the "underdeveloped" areas.

If the word "intelligentsia" itself is detached from

its connotation of "intelligence," it can be used to cover a broad social category quite irrelevant to personal acumen. I shall use the word to encompass writers, artists, engineers, journalists, and economists—in fact all the educated classes insofar as they specialize in abstractions. Plainly, it is the intellectuals who provide the initial contact with foreigners, both "official" foreigners and tourists.

What has characterized most Arabic-speaking intellectuals—"opinion-makers"—until recently is a curious mixture of sophistication and primitiveness —an instance of a broader category of behavior often summed up as "levantinism." A familiarity with current fashions, a knowledgeable allusiveness about happenings in the important places of the world, a nodding acquaintance with foreign ideas, a superficial intimacy with the attitudes of the cosmopolitan vanguard, an easy familiarity with chic innovations, and at the same time an absence of genuine intellectual roots, of genuine feelings and ideas of one's own—these traits would seem to make up a fair definition of "levantinism."

It is a natural enough phenomenon. In the shakeup of social values attendant on the enforced transition to a different lifestyle (with its concomitant abandonment of traditions and old-fashioned education), the initial generations making the big jump were necessarily trained first of all in the humanities—the easiest subjects to absorb and to make a showing in. In addition, professions like the law were the easiest springboards to livelihoods and careers in the new societies arising out of the debris of the old order. Intellectuals with a smattering of law and French verse began to proliferate, occupying center stage in all the countries where the pres-

ence of the West had the greatest impact—Algeria,
Morocco, Egypt, Syria, and Lebanon.

A characteristic mélange of fashionable ideas became the starting point for discussion and reflection
in the reviving centers of the Middle East and
North Africa. Thousands of young people sent off
to study abroad—in France, England, America, and
Germany—would pick up the fashionable ideas
there and take them back home, tinctured by their
own preoccupations. Their own impulses were generated most often by a sort of general misfittery
rooted in the chronic inability of the economy to
provide a livelihood for the numerous people
whose education was out of all proportion to any
conceivable job opportunities. Thus the articulation
of public opinions has found its matrix, since the
Second World War, in the ragtag and bobtail of
Western ideas encompassing various aspects of socialism and populism tinged by the nationalist
inflammation that became *de rigueur* with the establishment of Israel in 1948.

With respect to what was going on in Europe
and America, Arab intellectuals would know what
was being bruited about in the Western capitals;
their own interests would be expressed most fash-
ionably in the idiom of more or less fanatical nationalism, which just because it had not really
struck roots in the "masses" had to be harped on all
the more vigorously.

The intellectuals encountered by foreigners occupy an entirely peculiar situation at home. Where
the masses are steeped in ignorance—still overwhelmingly the case throughout the Arab world,
except for Lebanon and Israel—the acquisition of
an education is first of all the prerogative of the

upper or middle classes. On the other hand, anyone who has managed to acquire it moves thereby into the upper classes himself, regardless of economic status. Hence educated people tend to be unemployed in a country like Egypt, whose upper crust, against the background of a backward mass of workers and farmers, is relatively advanced. It is difficult to create jobs to absorb intellectuals.

This is no doubt the reason for the persistent phenomenon of the large class of educated idlers who socially belong to the upper strata but cannot in a tight economy find places commensurate with their education.

Thus they fall naturally into politics—the business of those without any business. But politics is also encumbered by a variety of obstacles. On the one hand the masses are hard to infect with political ideas, which in the Middle East as elsewhere are too abstract for people engaged in the drudgery of making a living. Conversely, the elite is suspicious of intellectuals and their radicalism per se. Thus, even in the political life that is the only channel open to the misplaced intellectual, there is just the same bottleneck. They are thrown upon themselves and those members of the rising generation who are treading the same path. Their numbers keep growing, but in an increasingly lopsided way.

Providing no outlet for their energies, it is just this gulf between the masses beneath and the rarefied summits of the elite that plunges the intelligentsia into political agitation and also constrains that agitation within a sterile and abnormally airless arena.

This may explain the mélange of intransigence of form and poverty of content that characterizes intellectual trends in postcolonial, still under-developed areas. It also explains, no doubt, some of the characteristics of the two "ideologies" that have been permeating Arabic-speaking society very noticeably since the First World War, and overwhelmingly since the Second—nationalism and socialism.

NATIONALISM

Perhaps "Pan-Arabism," an ambiguous slogan at one time fashionable for the movement of Arab unity aimed at all those conceived of as ethnically "Arab," has generated the greatest amount of heat. The movement to unite the "Arabs" has had, indeed, a checkered history.

The movement for Arab unity that had begun stirring before the Second World War could hardly be said to have made much headway. The various campaigns for independence in the Middle East and North Africa were aimed at securing independence for each specific country; despite the rhetoric made much of in the movement and on public occasions, there was no question of a merger between any actual Arab states. Indeed, the only formal expression ever given to the movement for Arab unity was made by the British when, at the instigation of Anthony Eden (now Lord Avon), the Arab League was founded during the war itself as a means of fighting Nazi Germany. With seven members at its founding, the Arab League has survived to this day, having added another thirteen states to its membership. It is a far cry from what Eden had envisioned.

If we look back at the emergence of the Arab national movement and set it in historical perspective, we can see that the outstanding fact about its historical matrix is that the very premise of the movement—the enormous number of speakers of Arabic—contains a contradiction.

As I have pointed out, the great conquests of the Muslim Arabs 1,300 years ago disseminated a language while failing to create a nation. A linguistically based nationalist movement within the bosom of medieval Islam was impossible. The "true Arabs," the Bedouin of the great tribes, retired to their deserts; the populations speaking Arabic were ruled by foreign soldiers.

The common assumption that "Arabs" came under foreign dominion only with the advent of the Ottoman Turks (1517–1917) about 450 years ago is grossly misleading. The peoples whose unification was to be solicited by a self-conscious concept in the twentieth century had had a lengthy series of foreign rulers long before, notably the Mamelukes, of much the same stock as the Turks, who governed Egypt and Syria long before the Ottomans (1250–1517). (These Mamelukes constituted a formidably efficient force for the time: One of the reasons Egypt for centuries has been superior to Iraq and Syria, both economically and culturally, in spite of the celebrated fertility of the latter two countries, was because the Mamelukes were able to spare Egypt the Mongol presence by overpowering a formidable Mongol army in 1260.)

In fact, down to the beginning of the nineteenth century, when Western Europeans broke the Ottoman hold on the eastern Mediterranean, all Arabic-speaking countries were under the thumb of corps of slave guards originating without exception outside the area. With nothing to bind them to the countries they governed, the slave guards naturally spent their entire time exploiting their charges and fighting one another. Not only did the incessant civil strife weaken these countries, but it also laid them wide open to incursions of the Bedouin, for whom weakened government was a natural target. This in turn had the effect of cutting down on agricultural activity; the fact that farmers would reduce their production as much as possible has in fact been responsible for the endemic malnutrition still a feature of the Middle East.

Yet despite the oppressive presence of the Ottoman Government, the concept of an Arab nation did not emerge until the First World War. Before then not a single independent state was in existence that used Arabic as its official language.

The emergence of distinct political entities presenting themselves to the world as "Arab" stems directly from two major political events: the Young Turkish upheaval of 1908 and, more especially, the emancipation of Arabic-speaking Asia by Allied arms during the First World War. Inspired by Woodrow Wilson, the broadcasting of the new principles of national independence by the Allies established the framework in the Middle East for a new sociopolitical concept—that of nation-states based on the official use of Arabic. This was reinforced—indeed, given a most potent dynamism—by the discovery during the First World War that oil had become the most important source of energy in the world.

It was in the twentieth century, accordingly, that an unforeseen product of the Muslim conquests could manifest itself. The dissemination of the Arabic language had called into being elements that now, centuries later, were to serve as the matrix for a new people—or at least, since the movement for Arab unity has not yet succeeded, the foreshadowing of such a people.

At first sight it might seem an easy task to unify the Arabic-speaking countries. The mere fact of the Arab past and the foundation of Islam would seem enough to bolster an ideal acceptable to almost all speakers of the language, with the exception, perhaps, of Jews and Christians. An authentically common origin would seem to be a natural way of implanting a pervasive sense of identity among the various Arabic-speaking societies.

Since Islam was in its beginnings a genuine Arab creation, it would be easy to say that in all the societies it touched, Islam established a similar emotional complex and similar values, superimposed on the normal differences due to geography, climate, social structure, and so on. Thus there has never been a Syrian, Iraqi, or Hijazi literature; anything written in Arabic can be claimed by all speakers of Arabic as their own. Negatively, of course, this is a way of indicating that none of the Arabic-speaking countries has attained its own fulfillment as a nation-state within its own borders.

But such an assessment of the forces at work would be naïve. It would be absurd, for instance, to refer to any common historical experience shared by Morocco, Egypt, and Yemen. Not only are the differences among them profound in their nature, but also, before the modern period, they had practically no interaction at all. Even when Islam was a vibrant reality, the Muslim states never acted in concert, even against the Crusaders. Politically,

Islam never duplicated its "ideological" homogeneity in any form of unification. During the past
thousand years, in fact, the various states that since
the Second World War have emerged as "Arab"
have been more or less insulated against each other.

Conditions vary greatly in the various Arabic-
speaking countries; it would be rash to generalize.
Before the Second World War, as I have indicated,
not many Arabic speakers in the eastern Mediterranean were touched even remotely by the concept
of nationalism; if it was a "cause" at all, it concerned only a small minority.

Egypt itself, the biggest Arabic-speaking country
and the one with the longest modern identity, was
almost entirely self-absorbed. No Egyptian at that
time would have dreamed of calling himself an
"Arab"; in Arabic the word itself still meant no
more than Bedouin. As for the Egyptian peasants
(90 per cent of the population), it would have been
impossible even to explain to them the turn of
events by which the "Arabs"—the Bedouin of the
great deserts, historically outsiders, even enemies—
were now to be equated with themselves—the peasants of the oldest country in the world.

Egyptian Christians—the Copts, the oldest Christian community in existence—also remained untouched by Arab nationalism throughout the nineteenth century and well into the twentieth. Their
own specific response to their Muslim milieu had
been like that of the Syro-Lebanese Christians—a
version of patriotism that would serve as a bridge
to the Muslim majority. But whereas the Syro-
Lebanese Christians had found in the cultivation of
Arabic a way of shaping an "Arab" nationality, the
Copts had rallied behind a "pharaonic" view of his-

tory that was intended to take in all Egyptians—Muslims and Copts alike—by linking them jointly to the ancient past of Egypt. This mythology, while even more artificial than most, could at least be said to repose on the incontestable fact of Egyptian antiquity. Until long after the Second World War it was to remain a focus for the national aspirations of many intellectuals, though the depressed situation of the population as a whole, to be sure, scarcely left much room for such fanciful extravagances.

In the Arabian Peninsula, Syria, and Iraq, the tug of Islam was still greater. As pious Muslims, the bulk of the population felt themselves to be members of the vast comity of Islam; within Islam, their local attachments were paramount. The very importance of Arabic precluded it from being the hallmark of anything so narrow as a mere "nation," in any case a concept entirely at odds with Islamic tradition. For Muslims, after all, what is paramount is Islam itself, which even in the modern period takes precedence over nationality. As late as 1928 it was possible for the founder of Saudi Arabia, the late King Ibn Saud, to say that he was a Muslim first and an Arab second. This attitude, essentially medieval, enabled him to take into his administration Muslims from all over—Iraq, Syria, Egypt—without its seeming odd. Egypt itself, to be sure, has more parochial views, befitting its relative modernity.

The Arabic-speaking Christians of the Fertile Crescent were themselves divided, for that matter, on this very issue. Though nationalism had come into the Muslim world, as I have indicated, via the Christian communities of Syria and Lebanon, it had not, after all, converted all Arabic-speaking Christians to nationalism. For instance, the Maronites of Lebanon, the oldest affiliate of the Vatican and under French sponsorship since the nineteenth century, were at first receptive to nationalism as a way out of their seclusion, but quickly recoiled into their traditional posture of self-defense vis-à-vis their Muslim environment; the spasmodic crises that have corroded the fabric of the Lebanese constitution in the past decade have merely consummated the isolation of the Maronites. Now that Muslims have become Arab nationalists too, and with the resurgence of Islam have thus become chauvinists in a dual sense, the Maronites could hardly benefit by a concept of nationalism based merely on language.

North Africa, too, remained entirely untouched by the nationalist movement before the Second World War, and indeed, for long afterward. The problems here confronting the intellectuals who were promoting Arab unification on a large scale were complicated, especially in Morocco, by the presence of a substantial Berber element. After an early conversion to Islam, they had lived in a close symbiosis with Arabs for centuries without ever merging with them as far as self-consciousness was concerned.

(The Berbers remain an anthropological mystery. Present in North Africa since the beginning of history, they seem to be related linguistically to the ancient Egyptians even though physically they are often tall, fair, and blue-eyed. Berber languages belong, with ancient Egyptian and its Coptic offspring, in the "Hamitic" family of languages.

The Berbers encountered by the Muslim Arabs

on their mass migration from Arabia were also camel-breeding nomads, much like the Bedouin themselves. They provided the Arab Muslim movement with the manpower needed to undertake the conquest of the Iberian Peninsula.)

Arabic, as the language of the religion and the *lingua franca* of a huge empire, was taken over by countless Berbers, especially in the big towns—a process that in our day has intensified. There still subsist, however, large segments of the rural and tribal population that cling to their own dialects. Indeed, the French attempted to ease their administrative problems by the classical device of emphasizing Berberdom in contrast with Arabdom, but without notable success. On the other hand, the French view was based on the Berber particularism that has hampered Arab unification. Even though Morocco has become an ally of its fellow "Arab" states, the hinterland is far from homogenized culturally.

There is nothing, to be sure, to prevent the ascription of homogeneity even to a past that lacked it; countless African subjects of France recited, together with the children of Polish and German immigrants, the opening lines of French history: "Our ancestors the Gauls . . ." But that in itself depends on the formation of a national consciousness in the present—such as the American patriotism cherished by the children of immigrants who regardless of where their real fathers came from can look up to the Founding Fathers as their own.

In the case of the interaction between Christian and Muslim self-consciousness in the formation of "Arab" national sentiment, the relationship to a "constructed past" for any particular country is

bound to mean to Muslims something different
from what it would to the Christians who were excluded from it for so long. If the "Arabs" themselves were to become a nation on the foundation of
a common language, they would still remain 90 per
cent Muslim; for Christians not to feel that numerical preponderance sociopolitically too would surely
imply the complete obliteration of a specifically
Muslim self-consciousness—a utopian prospect at
any time, and in our own day quite strikingly so.

In Syria, for instance—the birthplace of modern
Arab nationalism—the impact of Europe has forked
into antithetical tendencies—an emphasis on both
"Arab" nationalism and, conversely, the growth of
ethnic self-consciousness in the numerical minorities.

Thus there is a dialectical interaction between
local and global allegiances. The Christian minority
that played a cardinal role in the genesis of modern
Arab nationalism is now in a complex position, particularly since the Lebanese crisis of 1975–76
showed up the fragility of the Christian position in
a Muslim milieu. Many of them are having second
thoughts. Those whose religious feelings are still
strong are falling back on their own traditions;
many others—those who have become Marxist—
have shifted to "The Revolution" their hopes of
forming a Great Society in which they would find
their place on a footing of equality.

By heightening the importance of Arabic in fos-
tering the emotions linked to patriotism, the interaction between nationalism and Islam has had the
curious consequence—in an age when "modernism"
is sweeping the field—of giving the Quran a special
role. Despite the secularism that has been making

inroads on Islam for the past few generations, and despite, even, the fact that it no longer holds the religious imagination as it used to, the Quran is still the underlying factor of unification in the Muslim world.

More specifically, it is no doubt the unchallengeable influence of the Quran that has most prevented the rise of a spoken vernacular in place of the standard Arabic modeled on the Quran. Though the Arabic of the Quran has had scarcely any influence on actual literary composition—it is, perhaps, *too* inimitable—it remains as the paradigm of all written Arabic. The very mold of the classical language, it has had the most profound, quasipolitical effect in unifying a huge speech area that without the linchpin of a sacred book and standard language would no doubt be inundated by dialects.

Since the differences among the dialects are formidable—uneducated natives coming from, say, Iraq and Morocco are scarcely able to communicate with each other—it is plain that the acceptance throughout such a wide area of the Quran, held aloft as a beacon even if mere lip service is paid to it, has been an effective means of preserving linguistic unity.

What has happened in the modern era is that classical Arabic has served as the basis of a more or less literary medium that has evolved directly into the modern idiom of, for instance, the newspapers, which remain the greatest medium of mass communication. In this way, even though the Quran itself is totally beyond everyday use, concealed from ordinary attention by a dense smoke screen of veneration, it necessarily serves as the basis of education in Muslim countries, and all the more so in

Arabic-speaking countries. Even in the most progressive it is assiduously studied in elementary schools.

The classical language proper, to be sure, is practically unintelligible to Arabic speakers today. It is not so much that the language has changed as that the vocabulary and the themes are light-years removed from anything modern; the lexicographical effort involved in learning classical poetry restricts it to the domain of specialists.

At the same time, of course, it is one of the symbols held up by the enthusiastic propagators of the national myth of our own day: The abrupt emergence of Arabic as a cultivated idiom in the distant past is considered a sort of miracle in and for itself. Everyone educated in contemporary Arabic is heir to the voluminous productivity of the high periods of linguistic creativity that dates from the Middle Ages and covers an enormous area—indeed, the wide range of the civilization of the Middle Ages. This legacy is accompanied by an almost equally substantial corpus of belles lettres, still the idiom of cultivated Arabic today. In the modern era, the popularization or rather respectabilization of such ancient tales as *The Arabian Nights* or *The Romance of Antar* has provided the literary awareness of educated speakers with a vehicle for a feeling of cultural unity throughout the Arabic-speaking world. Because of this the classical language enjoys the support not only of conservative and religious diehards, but also of nationalistically minded groups in each country.

In its turn, to be sure, this has complicated the ferocious struggle between the classical language, overspreading the whole of the Arab world, and the teeming vulgar dialects that vary considerably from locality to locality in each country. The true field of the local dialects remains, very naturally, all aspects of art that impinge on popular life— radio, vaudeville, and humor sheets.

Thus in the modern era the mythologizing tendencies of modern language-building have had a massive base. Paradoxically, present-day Arab nationalists find it easy to skip over the millennium during which the Bedouin had withdrawn into the desert, leaving their language to evolve as the vernacular of a cosmopolitan society. Modern nationalists are unconsciously going all the way back to the earliest period of "Arab" solidarity—Bedouin self-consciousness vis-à-vis all non-Bedouin—and generalizing the unique contribution of the original Arabs to history—a world language and religion— to cover a situation in which the Arabic language is singled out as defining the heterogeneous society that speaks it.

(Socially, to be sure, the primacy of the Arabs was never wiped out—a pedigree going back if not to the Prophet's tribe at the very least to the four rulers of the first Caliphate is still a precious possession throughout Islam, even though biologically that primacy became meaningless very early on. Among the Bedouin, descent on the mother's side was just as important as on the father's, but since the establishment of the despotism in the early Caliphate, descent on the mother's side had no importance at all. Most of the caliphs' mothers were simply foreign slave girls.)

By the sixteenth century, when the Ottoman Turks united the whole of the Arabic-speaking belt —with the exception of Morocco, which was in no sense Arab—there was no expression of the "Arab spirit" left at all, except, precisely, in the free life

of the great Bedouin tribes of the Arabian Peninsula. They were in no way affected by the "Arab
spirit" themselves, and were also scarcely meddled
with at all by the Turks.

The only expression of the free life of the desert
that might be called Arab in a narrow ethnic sense
was the emergence in the eighteenth century of a
movement of Islamic fundamentalism in Arabia
linked to the name of Muhammad Abd al-Wahhab.
Entirely free of nationalist tendencies in its own
self-consciousness and preoccupied solely with the
cleansing of "corrupt" Islam by a return to the
pristine purity of its first period, this movement
was nevertheless to serve as the organizing principle
of the northern Bedouin and ultimately to give rise
to the modern dynasty of Saudi Arabia.

This in itself illustrates a curious paradox:
Though the Wahhabis were purely Arab, their
own preoccupation with the purification of Islam
made them Muslims first and foremost. In a round-
about way, accordingly, the political consciousness
of the Arabs as such, obliterated by the success of
their religion in its first phase, was restored a thousand years later by another religious movement in
Arabia, which once again served to give an "ethnic" definition to an Arab community in spite of its
own religious—that is, non-"ethnic"—principles.

What is perhaps most characteristic of the present-day concentration on Arab nationalism among
those who are tantalized by it is the degree to
which it represents a personal decision. In stable nationalities, as a rule, the individual is not called on
to make a *choice:* Born a Frenchman, a Frenchman
remains one, his personal interests as diversified as
he chooses to make them.

In the present-day Arab world, however, nationality is not yet stable; the decision as to whether to "be" an Arab is actually a matter of caprice; the individual can just as well choose to identify himself as an Egyptian or a Muslim. He can also add the word "Arab" to something else, even an antithetical concept, such as an "Arab Christian" instead of an "Arabic-speaking Phoenician." Though an Arabic-speaking Muslim has easier problems, it is just this element of personal voluntarism that is a source of torment for many minorities within the Arabic-speaking Muslim sphere, where self-identification, resting ultimately on language, must contend with many other vehicles of identity.

This homogeneous quality of Islamic civilization, seen from the outside, is actually rather misleading. The patina of sameness throughout Islam, including especially the Arabic-speaking sector, seems at first glance to bespeak an underlying unity. But the national, even the regional factors, against the background of extreme diversification of genesis, create a different picture. Islam was immensely successful in providing different elements with an overarching umbrella; the creation of an immense framework to encompass elements of diverse origin was no doubt its paramount achievement. Yet once they are looked for, the various influences surface immediately—the Jewish element, the Christian, the Hellenistic, the Persian; even a Hindu strand claims attention.

SOCIALISM

It is doubtless socialism, most flamboyantly in its Marxist version, that has proved to have been the most pervasively adopted Western idea in the Arab world, indeed, as it has been in the Third World as a whole.

There has been some confusion about the interaction of Islam and Marxism, especially when the version of Marxism is communism. Many scholars—the chief source of information, if only because of the difficulties of Arabic—have preserved a rather abstract attitude toward communism as a system of theory and Arab nationalism as a political movement. Preoccupied more by ideal concepts than by the play of real forces, scholars have found it easy to maintain that Islam by its very nature is immune to Marxist doctrine. This abstract attitude has gone in tandem with the even more abstract notion that Soviet policies derive their rationale from Marxism.

If these ideas had any substance it would be impossible to explain the influence of the Soviet Union in the Arab world. Yet it is obvious that the seizure of power by various juntas in the Middle East and North Africa has been brought about by a simple problem—how to industrialize a country lacking adequate capital. When the regimes of Egypt, Syria, Iraq, and Algeria were taken over by more or less professing socialists, preponderantly Marxists, the model they required stood ready-made before them—the Soviet executive, with its monopoly of foreign trade, its state economic planning, its crash industrialization programs, and its all-enveloping "ideology."

It was an admirable model that allowed a small group of people to take power in a backward area by radically overhauling the economy, or seeming to do so. Since practical problems are far more difficult to solve than problems of mystique, ideology, public appearances, and "drive," it was natural for such leaderships to compensate with propaganda what they could not accomplish in fact. The Soviet dictatorship has provided an ensemble of institutions enabling the youthful leaders of the underdeveloped nations to display their initiative by vast programs of "reform"—that is, economic expansion—clinging to power while paying lip service to the collective mystique justifying their ambitions.

None of this, plainly, has anything to do with the abstract affinity between Islam and Marxism. For that matter, even from the point of view of Islamic institutions themselves, it must be recalled that Islam since its inception has been grounded in the triple foundation of theocracy (a central sovereignty with a divine sanction), the army (the basic organization of Islam during its first few centuries), and the intelligentsia (the former bureaucracy of the scribes, inherited from Persia and Byzantium, plus the clergy). This is easily recognizable as the very model of Soviet authority itself: the element of divine sanction is organically replaced by the sacrality ascribed to the leaders' interpretation of Marxism (an interpretation, moreover, that is rammed home by the police force).

The two great successes of Marxism—the Soviet Union and China—have had a stunning effect on the emotions and ideas of the intelligentsia from Morocco to Iraq.

From a purely intellectual point of view it might seem obvious, perhaps, that, whatever one may think of Marxism as a doctrine, its validity would seem to have been destroyed by precisely these "successes," which contradict very neatly all the principles attributed to Marxism in theory.

From the point of view of the founders of Marxism, the development of capitalism was to lead to conditions where more and more people grew poorer and poorer while fewer and fewer people grew richer and richer, thus giving rise to an infuriated proletariat disciplined by factory routine. Prepared by capitalist technology for the transition to an economy of abundance, the infuriated proletariat easily takes power, since by virtue of capitalist evolution, it has become the predominant element in society. Thus would be inaugurated the socialist age.

It is very evident that what happened in Russia was just the opposite of this. There a handful of men made a *putsch* in a few hours, and to keep themselves in power erected repressive machinery of matchless ferocity. In China, which had practically no proletariat at all, it proved possible for the Marxist leaders to declare blandly that it was the peasantry—for Marx and Engels the epitome of the petty bourgeoisie—who had to conduct the revolutionary struggle for a socialist society.

Yet it was precisely an unforeseen by-product of the Marxist movement—repression and regimentation on a titanic scale—that was to be the chief factor in the spread of Marxist ideas. It was orthodoxy that suppressed opposition and welded together the following of the Marxist governments; it was orthodoxy, institutionalized as an expression of state power, that gained partisans even in areas not subject to force. Marxism became, in fact, another religion, or at least another intellectual fashion—

enhanced by the glamour of power. Ideas were well-nigh irrelevant.

Thus, in the Middle East and North Africa, Marxism, stripped of what had been its intellectual pretensions before its accession to power, became a cluster of watchwords that could galvanize a small elite. Though Marxism, despite its "scientific" claims, gives no guidelines for action or even for its own interpretation, it does justify both paranoid exclusiveness and force. Hence numerous groups tinged by both Marxism and nationalism have sprung up throughout the Arab world, except where specifically proscribed, as in such traditionalist monarchies as Saudi Arabia, and sporadically in Egypt. In Syria, Iraq, Lebanon, Egypt, Algeria, Libya, and Morocco, and for that matter even in the Sudan (outstandingly backward from all points of view), there are small coteries of intellectuals grappling with the various problems posed by the taking of power in countries even more unsuited for socialism than were Russia and China.

With respect to the intelligentsia, these factors have given rise to an extreme instance of fashionable levantinism, made all the more possible since Marxism itself, in its systematic simplification and sloganization by vast governments, has become a popular panacea. As a topic of conversation, a rhetorical style, it can be utilized by anyone with the "gift of gab" or even, more simply, a knack for social conformism. If even the French intelligentsia, after all, has taken over Marxism as summed up in a few catchwords, how can it fail to tantalize countries just evolving into the modern world?

When meeting intellectuals in the Arab world,

accordingly, foreigners will notice a strangely fluent, catchy, even glib rehearsal of recurrent themes. In the first five minutes they will see that the recurrence of such themes is their most general feature. They will find a huge amount of talk revolving around a few simple notions—"imperialism," "Arab socialism," "taking power," "annihilating the Zionist-imperialist invaders," "planning a new society." Nor will these slogans vary much, indeed, from those current in the innumerable coteries that have come under Marxist influence all over the world. Since the headquarters of such slogans are now centered in the capitals of the Soviet Union and China, the simplification that has already been achieved in contemporary versions of Marxism can be given great flexibility and impact.

Concretely, the socialist movement in the Arab world scored a series of victories beginning in 1956, when nearly all Arabic-speaking countries, with the exception of the monarchies around the Persian Gulf, followed Egypt toward some form of socialism. It was around that time that the example of the Soviet Union, with its endless chain of "Five-year Plans," was followed. One parvenu socialist or semisocialist regime after another, full of high hopes for the renovation of the economy via planning, started its own series of global plans, accompanied by varying schemes of land reform as a way of ending feudal exploitation. On the other hand, no attempt has as yet been made to accompany this rash of socialist planning by an actual abolition of capitalism altogether.

In a way, despite the heated rhetoric of Arab leaders, socialism on a global scale—that is, as a restructuring of the world via the abolition of "capitalism" and the installation of comprehensive institutions such as those of the Soviet Union and China—has not really been attempted. Instead, empirically grounded, piecemeal measures have been applied, perhaps because of the only too obvious difficulties that weigh down Marxist governments like the Soviet and the Chinese, and the inability of basically feeble regimes to imitate them. There may also be a tacit admission of Islam's basic aversion to socialism as such, accompanied, perhaps, by an appreciation that there is something hollow, after all, in Marxist pretensions.

This has not, to be sure, had the smallest effect on the torrent of government rhetoric in the Arab socialist countries. Rhetorically, at least, the radio stations and government-controlled press in Iraq, Syria, Algeria, and South Yemen sound flamboyantly and uncompromisingly fanatical; they remain archsocialist in propaganda while shrugging aside any suggestion that they live up to their theories. The "Ba'ath," a movement at the helm of both Syria and Iraq—which nevertheless are at loggerheads with each other on all major questions—is a splendid example of socialist partisans who without doing anything to implement socialism nevertheless hew to a single line with respect to foreign policy. To outsiders it is clear that a rhetorical ideal has been set up, a beacon for public opinion, so that a small vocabulary of epithets can do yeoman service as a lever for the manipulation of appearances. All enemies of the government spokesman are simply called "reactionaries," lackeys of the imperialists, friends of Zionism, and so on. For the Syrian Ba'athists, as well as for the Iraqi, Marxism has long since become a mere stylistic mannerism, as it has, to be sure, in the Soviet Union and China too. In the Arab world, of course, there can be no question of large-scale socialist or socialist-sounding enterprises; hence not even an institutional substructure is present to be camouflaged by the rhetoric.

Marxism has also inspired the activities of the non-Jordanian Palestinian Arabs, reduced to terrorism by their incapacity to gain a large enough following to influence events otherwise. Algeria's Marxists are enthralled by the possibilities of large-scale state planning. Libya's President Qaddafi, wildly eccentric, has his own mixture of socialism and Muslim fundamentalism. Egypt's President Sadat, involved more directly in genuine state problems, has modified very substantially his predecessor's somewhat naïve views of socialist transformation. Egypt is now returning, in fact, to a moderate form of mixed economy that by now characterizes in any case the bulk of the countries of the world outside the downright Marxist sector; in the autumn of 1975 Sadat signaled an abrupt reversal of his pro-Soviet stand by coming to an informal accord with Iran and Saudi Arabia against the spread of Soviet influence.

With Marxism, attenuated or not, as the official style of expression in the Middle East regimes outside the monarchies, everyone in power is likely to encase himself in some "uncompromising" position while camouflaging his real interests. This is, of course, no more than a further illustration of what I have pointed out: Just as rhetoric replaces substance, so propaganda replaces realism. A Cabinet meeting, for instance, will vote to dispatch troops or money to a brother country in distress. The vote will be publicized with fanfare—Arab honor has been satisfied. That will be the end of it—neither troops nor money will actually be dispatched— the vote has taken the place of a fact.

(This tendency is highlighted by a true story: A missionary is testing Muslim Arabs' reactions to the New Testament. In a famous parable [Mt. 21:28], one son assents to his father's request without doing anything about it, while the other son refuses, verbally, but carries out the request anyhow. Generally the Muslim Arabs thought the first son's behavior better—it showed more *respect*.)

The Syrian socialist regime—the Ba'ath—is grounded in close relations with the Soviet Union and the "people's democracies." Some big dams have been built; the United States has been denounced with unflagging venom. Yet governmental uniformity does nothing but use Ba'athist rhetoric to camouflage the same old factional spirit. There is an immense proliferation of tendencies and allegiances, all inside the Ba'ath: conservatives, Muslim Brethren, pro-Egyptian, pro-Chinese, pro-Soviet factions. Yet they are *all* Ba'athists—in appearance.

In this way what might have been an open conflict, even a bloody war, has been transformed into a blurred, confused, backstage contest of coteries. It makes it impossible to assess the actual strength of the Ba'ath. This spectrum of political impulses that merely cancel each other precludes a cohesive government policy; action is short-circuited, sabotaged, neutralized, nullified.

This is one more illustration of the magnetic effect on Arabs of appearances for their own sake. In this one respect what goes on in all socialist Arab countries is much the same—in Algeria as well as in

Iraq and Syria, the fashionable vocabulary pays lip service to collective ideals, whatever they may be, without making an effort to achieve whatever the ideals stand for. Consciences are appeased, realities are accommodated; idealism, on the surface, glows.

It was entirely typical that Syria, the most rabidly anti-Israeli regime—if shadings in rhetoric can be accurately assessed—did not participate at all in the Six-day War of June 1967 but kept its armies safely rooted outside the Damascus gates.

It is this elephantiasis of rhetoric that has, no doubt, enabled normal life to go on beneath the façade of official pronouncements. It is still possible to "do business" not only in Morocco, Saudi Arabia, Kuwait, and Tunisia, but even in countries where capitalism is frowned on, such as Syria, Iraq, Libya, and Algeria—where one might have thought that those at the national helm, ostensibly world reformers, would simply have wiped out all private enterprise.

Yet even though private enterprise has been put under restrictions, it is still entirely viable. In the case of the big oil-exporting countries, to be sure, the very nature of the monopoly has imposed state capitalism on the country; perhaps the notion of middle-class entrepreneurism has been outmoded more uniformly in the Middle East and North Africa than elsewhere.

Still, in spite of everything, things remain fluid. Even Egypt, the most influential Arabic-speaking country, has begun to show serious lapses from the somewhat primitive ideal of land reallocation and national state planning held aloft by the late Gamal Nasser. If state planning has been a catastrophe for the Soviets, with their vast resources and blanket ferocity, how much the more so must it have been for Egypt, with quite inadequate technical personnel and no resources to speak of?

The wobbliness of the Egyptian economy can hardly be overestimated. In some ways Egypt entered the modern age before many other countries. Railways were established long before they were in many places in Europe, and the application of perennial irrigation through barrages, canals, and pumps, as well as the creation of the Suez Canal, placed Egypt well athwart the most forward-looking elements of the modern age.

But the lengthy British occupation, which took advantage of the climate and of the Nile to turn Egypt into a great cotton center, at the same time restricted its potentialities, which in turn were limited to a very narrow base. It must be recalled that though Egypt looks quite big on the map, its habitable area is no more than about twelve thousand square miles (about the size of New Jersey or Wales), only a little bigger than Israel. The habitable land comprises only some 3.5 per cent of the total area.

But with a population now edging up toward the forty million mark, the woes of Egypt beggar belief. Almost 60 per cent of the peasantry is nearly constantly immersed in Nile water; this leads to endemic diseases that are scarcely controllable, such as bilharzia and hookworm. The conjunction of these two debilitating diseases means that countless adults spend their lives in a constant state of exhaustion and anemia, added to widespread chronic malaria, numerous eye diseases, chronic malnutrition, and other deficiency diseases that make diarrhea one of the commonest causes of death. Even though Egypt now graduates three times as many physicians as it did twenty years ago, the total today comes to only fifteen hundred a year, a long jump from what is needed. The Aswan High Dam, which it had been hoped would increase the tillable land by 40 per cent, may still do so, but meanwhile the population has gone up by 50 per cent since the dam was projected.

The problems of Egypt are, to be sure, unique, both because of their scope and because of the size of the population. But all the Arab states confront a huge cluster of afflictions. Emerging as articulated structures, the local regimes have been so entangled in the endless complexities of adjusting to the modern era—poverty, illiteracy, disease, social frictions, debasement of public life—that it seemed as though all their energies might well be taken up by practical tasks. After all, though the extent of the oil reserves of the Middle East was still not established, there could be no doubt that they were substantial; for some countries, at least, the light at the end of the tunnel might seem to be an oil burner.

Yet politics overshadowed all developments; perhaps inevitably, the leaderships of the various countries were to become embroiled in a conflict that, still going strong, was to involve very nearly all of them in varying degrees—the seemingly intractable imbroglio with Israel.

VI

The Response to Israel—and to Oil

Hampered from the outset by the difficulty of reconciling the Jewish National Home with the mounting protests of the local inhabitants, the Palestine Mandate was giving the British Government a virulent headache; it had been growing steadily worse from the early twenties on. This was compounded in 1945 by the paramount resolve of the British Government, led by the Labor Party, to liquidate the British Empire as rapidly as possible.

The Zionist community itself was feeling the impact, both moral and material, of the catastrophe that had befallen European Jewry at the hands of the Nazis and their collaborators in Europe—a catastrophe that had wiped out some six million Jews, a third of the whole people. In Palestine the pressure to house the survivors of the Nazi death camps became more and more urgent.

Confronted by this same pressure, the British Government decided to drop the whole tangle. Making somewhat hasty preparations to evacuate the area two years after the end of the war, it seems the British Labor leaders went about it in the conviction that what had become an unmanageable problem for them would be solved by the forces of history.

Trans-Jordan, still under the same Mandate as those parts of Palestine west of the Jordan and defended by the Arab Legion under the command of a British officer (Glubb Pasha), was thought capable of cutting the ground from under the Zionist Jewish community of western Palestine. This would create a new entity deprived, very naturally, of the control of immigration and land purchase that had been in Zionist hands and hence easily integratable with the Arab environment.

As a way out of the impasse, a commission of inquiry was appointed; it came up with proposals for partitioning the country into a Jewish and an Arab section. When a resolution along these lines was passed by the United Nations organization formed at the end of the war, it was accepted by the Zionist representatives, but the Arab representatives, considering the proposals inequitable, rejected them, and were outvoted.

The upshot was the formation of the State of Israel. The hasty British evacuation of the area seems to have been based on the expectation of a collapse of the embryonic Jewish state. Unformed, but in a way highly organized, the Zionist community had been fighting its own struggle for self-affirmation for years; during the war it had perfected its organizations both for defense and for opposition to the mandatory power. But now it faced armies of five neighboring states—Egypt, Jordan, Syria, Iraq, and Lebanon.

In the somewhat chaotic fighting that instantly broke out, the Arab leaders in Palestine, encouraged by their military allies, made extravagant promises to the effect that it would be only a matter of days before the Jews were entirely wiped out and the land returned to its rightful inhabitants. As a result, a stream of Muslims and Christians, thinking they would be away from home for only a few days before the armies of the five countries won a smashing victory, took to their heels for Jordan, Syria, and Lebanon in a mass flight based on not much more than a combination of hysteria and overoptimism.

Some half a million people left their homes in the hope of a rapid victory; a generation later they and their descendants were still constituting a first-class "refugee problem." It must be emphasized, however, that, for most of these fugitives, leaving their homes meant no more than removing themselves a few miles to villages and families of kindred religion in a different section of a large territory that had always been just as heterogeneous as Palestine itself. But because of the way the war developed the Muslims and Christians who had fled the war zone were unable to integrate themselves in their new communities.

What happened in the frantic though short-lived war that established Israel as an independent state was to have repercussions that are still with us. The Jewish Israelis—as they are now to be called—had naturally hoped that once established, the new state would somehow be accepted not only by the world community—the United States and the Soviet Union recognized it at once—but, far more important, by the neighboring states too. The Jewish Israelis were convinced that once presented with a *fait accompli*, the soberer heads among the leaders of the Arab states and of Egypt (which participated in the war out of sympathy but still regarded itself as essentially non-Arab) would bow to the inevitable, and eventually all would be well.

Arab resistance, however, proved to be obdurate. Iraq and Syria, led by various Marxist coalitions, and Lebanon, whose delicate balance was at risk, followed the Muslim consensus. Egypt, at first indifferent to the emotional issues involved in the war, was transformed in 1953 into a dictatorship headed by Nasser, whose single-party regime was soon to be dedicated to a massive socio-economic overhaul accompanied by a fateful shift in self-image.

Two years after taking power, Nasser announced that he was no longer merely an Egyptian or a Muslim leader, but was, on the contrary, essentially the leader of the Arab world as part of his leadership of all Islam. Thus, the fact that Egypt had been both Muslim and Arabic-speaking for a thousand years enabled Nasser to present himself as something no Egyptian past or present had ever even dreamed of.

To be sure, his *démarche*, a bolt from the blue for any knowledgeable observer, had a certain plausibility about it. In the West, of course, the plausibility was, so to speak, a foregone conclusion. Westerners naturally tend to lump together all speakers of the same language as the same people, which generally, after all, they are. Exceptions like the Swiss and Belgians are rare. Thus it was natural for Westerners, whose knowledge of the area was in

any case generally limited, to take in their stride a
fact that remains most remarkable.

In its millennial history as a Muslim nation,
Egypt had never once been referred to as "Arab";
during its hundred and fifty years as a modern nation-state it has never been anything but Egyptian,
while, as I have indicated, its reaction to the attrac-
tion of present-day nationalism took the explicitly
"pharaonic" form of pride in the six thousand years
of its past.

With respect to the Arab-Israeli conflict, in any
case, Nasser's proclamation of Egypt as a leader of
Arabdom was to inject a weighty factor into the
tussle. By ranging itself ardently on the side of the
Arabs and then by superimposing on the allegiance
a new factor of "national" commitment, Egypt
made all positions jell into an antagonism that is still
intense.

The Egyptian leaders felt "humiliated" at being
defeated with their allies in 1948 by such a puny
state as Israel, and committed themselves to what
even then looked like a drawn-out war. Moreover,
Nasser already had his hands full, having taken on
the task of solving Egypt's countless problems—endemic diseases of all kinds, a huge birth rate, general illiteracy, the absence of a genuine industrial
plant, and overdependence on a limited agriculture
and a lack of basic resources.

Precisely this plethora of insoluble problems
may, to be sure, explain the new commitment of
Egypt to its "fellow Arabs," for the involvement in
the conflict with Israel was part and parcel of a
general shift in the world balance of power. Egypt
could thus offer its assistance to a new power now

surfacing in force throughout the Middle East—the Soviet Union.

After unprecedented bloodletting, the Soviet Union had emerged intact from the Second World War. In the face of American apathy and general withdrawal, the Soviet executive was strategically situated to exploit the possibilities afforded by its role as beacon to the "underdeveloped" and "emerging" peoples. As the British began withdrawing, the Soviets began moving into the eastern Mediterranean and the Persian Gulf. Frustrated in an initial attempt to envelop Iran via a "mass movement" (Tudeh) in 1946, Stalin took advantage of the British difficulties with Israel in 1947–48 to give Israel some support, allowing them some arms via Czechoslovakia and sponsoring at the UN the establishment of the State of Israel in 1948.

The moment the British had actually withdrawn, however, Stalin's policy veered. Always cautious, he now became the patron of Arab "national" aspirations. When John Foster Dulles, the U. S. Secretary of State, upset Egyptian-American relations in 1956 by suddenly abandoning the American subsidy of a much-wanted dam at Aswan, he enabled Nasser to swerve away from his dependence on the West, especially the United States, and to develop a strategy of far greater flexibility through a special relationship with the Soviet Union.

In 1956 this began to pay off. Nasser, with the massive support of the Soviet Government, established a major buildup of armed forces in the Sinai Peninsula and advertised his intention to crush the Israeli army and smash the State of Israel. Nevertheless, the Israelis, in conjunction with France and Great Britain, who were both irritated by

Nasser's unilateral nationalization of the Suez Canal earlier in the year, went into dramatic action. The Egyptian, Syrian, Jordanian, and Iraqi armies were routed; the Israelis advanced into Sinai and were on the verge, moreover, of moving into Jordan.

Both Great Powers intervened. With a maximum of solemnity and lethal chilliness, both President Eisenhower and Premier Khrushchev admonished the Israelis, British, and French to cease all action forthwith on pain of armed intervention. The nerves of the Israeli leadership, like those of their British and French allies—an unlikely alliance to begin with—snapped; they gave in at once. The status quo was more or less restored. Indeed, Nasser, whom one might earlier have thought to have suffered a potentially harmful military defeat, recovered more through the ensuing diplomacy than he had lost in the battle. Committed more than ever to a policy of intransigence regarding Israel, the Nasser regime sat even more firmly in the saddle than before, if only because the Soviets seemed to be conspicuously treating Nasser and other Arab leaders as allies of consequence.

Plainly, none of the Arab governments surrounding Israel could accept Israel as an integral part of the environment. The elites of all Arabic-speaking countries, both of the traditional Muslim states like Saudi Arabia and Yemen, together with the parvenu regimes of Marxists or socialists, as in Syria and Iraq, had become inflamed by a fervor strangely disproportionate to the true issues involved.

Moreover, the contagion of a new patriotism had spread throughout North Africa. The French, running into difficulties with their own empire much like those of the British, collided with the independence movements of Tunisia, Algeria, and Morocco; within the space of a few years all had manged to shake off the French presence. Under De Gaulle, France gave up all its material props and withdrew to a position of exclusively spiritual authority. In addition, a *putsch* in the huge, empty country of Libya put another dictator on the scene, Muammar Qaddafi. As soon as it became clear that Libyan oil reserves were even greater than had been foreseen, Qaddafi could move into the forefront of charismatic world leaders.

Thus all the diverse countries of the Arab world, all now members of the Arab League, could unite *de facto* in a general determination to destroy the Israeli state. Israel's sole prop throughout this period was the allegiance of the American Jewish community and of the Jews in France and Great Britain, along with the sponsorship of the United States administration, which has repeatedly reaffirmed its support for Zionist aspirations ever since the First World War.

THE RECENT CRISES

The last two phases of the Arab-Israeli conflict set the scene for the present conjuncture.

In June 1967 Israel responded to Nasser's blockade of the Tiran Staits by launching an attack, mainly on the air force of Egypt, but also making a massive onslaught this time on Jordan and Syria. The concerted action was remarkably successful. In the space of six days the Israelis wiped out the Egyptian air force and occupied the whole of the Sinai Peninsula, the Gaza Strip, the whole of the West Bank of the Jordan, as well as the eastern sections of Jerusalem and the Golan Heights of Syria. As the Israelis set about exploiting their much-improved position, they could breathe more easily. They could now regard the Sinai Peninsula as a priceless buffer against any future attack from Egypt; the Golan Heights could play the same role for Syria.

The West Bank itself, to be sure, was more than a mere piece of territory; though of emotional importance to Jews—it comprises ancient Samaria and Judea—it was densely settled by Arabs, few of whom could, no doubt, be regarded as Israeli partisans. In spite of themselves, the Israelis had added a substantial bloc of at best apathetic or downright hostile Arabs to those already under their administration.

The most recent phase of the Arab-Israeli conflict brought about a situation whose outcome is not yet consolidated. What was quickly referred to as the "Yom Kippur War" of October 1973 showed for the first time a definite advance in the ability of the Arab countries to organize themselves.

Equipped with vast amounts of Soviet military weapons of the most sophisticated kind, as indeed they had been in 1956 and 1967, the armies of Egypt and Syria concerted a major onslaught on Israel that from their point of view looked very promising—for a few days. Having achieved an unusual element of surprise, the Egyptian-Syrian armies advanced very quickly both in the north of Israel and in the Sinai Peninsula, and seemed about to smash through the desperate rally made by the Israeli army. Yet the rally proved successful; a few days later the Israeli army made a remarkable comeback

—so effective, indeed, that it forced its way deep into Egyptian territory. The Israeli army was on the verge of encircling a major portion of the Egyptian army when it was held back by a joint action of the sponsors of the two sides of the conflict, respectively—the Soviet Union and the United States.

The United States administration, in accordance with its own strategic view of its general relations with the Soviet Union, thought it politic to restrain the Israelis from a victory in order to allow the Egyptian regime of Anwar Sadat to retain its authority and thus serve as a party to an eventual settlement. The chain of negotiations, counternegotiations, counterclaims, and propaganda, guided on the American side by Henry Kissinger, the Secretary of State, came to a conclusion in September 1975: Israel and Egypt agreed on a settlement in the Sinai Peninsula in which, in return for a substantial clearing of the strategically important Mitla and Gidi passes and a restoration of the Abu Rudeis oil fields to Egypt, relations between the two countries were to be relatively normalized. American civilian monitors—two hundred—were to be interposed in Sinai between the forces on both sides to supervise the "early warning" installations.

The settlement of 1975, though far from formal peace, may mark a break in the Arab front against Israel and a new orientation of Egypt and Saudi Arabia, which in conjunction with Iran have broken out of the pro-Soviet camp.

The Soviet investment in Egypt—many billions of dollars—has simply been lost.

THE PALESTINE LIBERATION
ORGANIZATION

The Six-day War of 1967 cast into high relief an entirely new ingredient in the Middle East tangle: the Palestine Liberation Organization. A coalition of disparate groups, of varying mixtures of Marxism and nationalism, its pre-eminence is mainly the result of the general pressure against Israel as buttressed by the immense oil resources of some Arab states. Estimated as encompassing some twelve thousand people, the PLO enjoys an income reputed to run about $150 million a year, mainly derived from Saudi Arabia.

The PLO was launched in 1964 in order to harass the "reactionary" Arab regimes as part of the general campaign being carried on by the "progressive" regimes. At first, accordingly, the PLO agitated for the ousting of King Hussein of Jordan: Since Jordan had been dislodged by the Israelis from ancient Samaria and Judea—the "West Bank" —it was easy to present this defeat as a betrayal, or at the very least incompetence, on the part of Hussein, and to demand the reorganization of Jordan and Israel alike under the authority of the PLO.

For a few years the hostility between Hussein and the PLO, headed by Yasir Arafat, almost overshadowed the conflict with Israel itself. Operating from Beirut, its headquarters since 1966, the PLO kept up a campaign of agitation in Jordan that came to a violent end in September 1970, when the main component of the PLO, Arafat's Fatah, was suppressed after a massacre of hundreds and the PLO retreated *en bloc* to Beirut.

After the 1973 war with Israel, however, a conference of Arab leaders in Rabat, Morocco, declared the PLO the sole representative of the "Palestinians" everywhere. This victory for Arafat was consummated by his reception in the General Assembly of the United Nations, which also passed a resolution denouncing Zionism as "racism" in 1975; in January 1976 the Security Council accepted the PLO as a party to its discussion of the Middle East imbroglio.

The presence of the PLO in Lebanon seems to have triggered the civil war that began raging there in 1975. Lebanon, based on a constitutional arrangement that gave the ancient Christian community—mainly the Maronites—a slight priority in the government, was torn to pieces in the violence that broke out between the Maronites and their allies and a coalition of radical "Palestinians" and Muslims sponsored at first by the Syrian regime of Hafez Assad. The civil war, which killed tens of thousands of people on both sides, ended with the breakup of the alliance between Syria and the "Palestinians" in Lebanon. Syria, whose private faction within the PLO, the Saiqa, had been unable to help it control the turbulent arena, intervened in Lebanon in 1976 directly, making Lebanon, in effect, a protectorate. To avoid alarming the Israelis excessively, Syria kept this development within the forms of diplomacy. The PLO, through its base in Lebanon, collided directly with the Syrian government; its role within the rivalries splitting the Arab world was profoundly affected.

Yet the PLO, despite all vicissitudes in Lebanon,

remains the obvious protagonist, on the Arab side, in the handling of the problem of Israel. It is the only element that can claim to represent, on the basis of philosophic principle, a movement aimed *openly* at the extinction of Israel. And the thrust of this philosophic principle was derived from the emergence, in the wake of the Six-day War of 1967, of the "Palestinian nation."

The inhabitants of Palestine, who had hitherto been called either Christians or Muslims, or by some specifically ethnic designation, or, more generally, "Arabs"—in accordance both with traditional European usage and with the modern propaganda of Arab unity—now came to be called "Palestinians." The name embodied not only the traditional geographical sense, but, far more important, all the emotive connotation of nationalist feeling. The mere fact of the use of the word as a collective designation of the inhabitants of Palestine who were not Jews served to fix it gradually in public consciousness as the designation of an ethnic group whose rightful territory could now be considered that which was appropriately called Palestine. An instance of nominalism at its most persuasive, the new designation thus represented a confluence between a geographical term and a concept of statehood, both fused in the projection of an irredenta linked to an ideology.

This conception has been remarkably successful. The well-known fact that no such people as the "Palestinians" had ever existed proved to be incapable of counteracting its rapidly spreading influence. Infused now with emotion, the word "Palestinian," epitomizing a new concept of state-nation, could rally support for a small group presenting itself as the spokesmen of a movement.

Thus, by creating well-nigh overnight the notion of a people who had been ejected from their own land and by securing the support of some of the great factors involved in the Arab-Israeli conflict— the other Arab countries; the "emerging" African countries; and above all, the Soviet bloc and China (with their countless adherents, partisans, dupes, and agents throughout the world)—the PLO succeeded in upsetting the foundation of the Jewish state.

The shift in focus with the emergence of the new concept of a "Palestinian people," as distinct from a conglomerate of disparate communities merely located in Palestine, radically altered the balance of forces. Since the Six-day War the Israelis have had to wage a struggle against the admission of this concept into discussion, since in its very nature it entails the dissipation of their fundamental claim to the territory they are settled on. This is all the more obvious because of the inroads made by the concept of a "Palestinian nation" not merely on countless outsiders, including liberals in the United States and elsewhere who may be sincerely sympathetic to the existence of Israel, but also on many Jews, even on many Zionists.

For if the concept of a unitary, self-aware, and striving nation of "Palestinian Arabs" is accepted, if the countless denominational, social, and political differences that have fragmented the Arabic-speaking populations of the Middle East for more than a millennium are simply disregarded, and if the claim of the "nation" to its own land is accepted, there is plainly no place at all for Israel as a state.

From just this public-relations point of view

there is an additional irony in the success of the PLO in parading as the spokesman of the "Palestinian nation." It is taking advantage, somewhat tardily, of a trap that the Zionist leadership of the twenties and thirties may be said to have set for itself.

Vexed by the exclusion of Trans-Jordan from the land-settlement clauses of the British Mandate for Palestine, the Zionist leaders thought it politic not to press the British too hard, especially in view of the difficulty of bringing about a massive Jewish immigration into Palestine. Presenting an appearance of moderation, they began using the word "Palestine" as though it referred only to the part of Palestine still open to the Jewish National Home. That moderation is now being paid for: The very word "Palestine" has become sufficiently blurred in the minds of a big public to enable Arab spokesmen to act as though Palestine were now *only* the section of the British Mandate now occupied by the successor State of Israel.

An ironic conclusion to Zionist optimism! The Zionist movement had been, in fact, relatively unprepared for the degree of resistance it encountered on Palestinian terrain. It had been very nearly a cliché before the First World War and even after that since the area as a whole was underpopulated, and since the ethnic consciousness of the population was not centered in Palestine, there would be no fundamental opposition. The inhabitants of Palestine, subjects of the Ottoman Empire, were divided into various Christian and Muslim sects that owed allegiance either to the broad communities of which they were fragments, or, in the geographical sense, to these communities as constituted over the much larger area of Syria—of which Palestine, both historically and administratively, merely constituted the southern extremity.

Hence, since Zionist aims were focused exclusively on the Holy Land, a small fragment of historic Syria (and *a fortiori* of the Arabic-speaking world as a whole), it had seemed reasonable to assume that the patriotism of the inhabitants of Palestine was directed either at the great expanse of Syria or, in the case of Pan-Arabs, at the endless reaches envisaged as the home of the newly projected Arab people.

In effect, the general movement for Arab nationalism reinforced this notion. As the movement increased gradually in strength in the aftermath of the Second World War, it could even be taken, in a way, as reinforcing the possibility of a peaceable outcome to the whole conflict generated by Zionism. For even though the campaign for Arab nationalism no doubt was bound to oppose the settlement of strangers on historically "Arab" lands, those lands were so spacious that from the point of view of equity—at least as understood by those outsiders—a persuasive case could be made to the effect that what the Zionists were claiming was a mere bagatelle.

After all, the Zionists and their partisans could say, the Arabian Peninsula (including Iraq, Syria, Lebanon, Jordan, and Palestine) is about 1,000,000 square miles. If one goes on to include the eastern Arab world as a whole (adding Egypt, the Sudan, and Libya), we arrive at a total of 3,271,308 square miles—an area equal to that of the United States. If we then go farther, as the Arab nationalist movement was to do a little later, to encompass Tunisia,

Algeria, Morocco, and the other members of the Arab League, we bring in more than another million square miles, for a total of 5,000,000. Against this staggering figure the "notch" reserved for Israel—10,000 square miles, less than 20 per cent of the original British Mandate for Palestine—seems laughably negligible.

Further, if we recall that almost 1,000,000 Jews, roughly 1 per cent of the population of Arabdom, were expelled from Arabic-speaking countries in the wake of the 1948 war, there might seem to be a rough justice in a territorial claim to 1 per cent of the total area of Arabdom—that is, 50,000 square miles, which amounts, very tidily, to the area of the original British Mandate. Against that the 10,000 square miles of present-day Israel would seem quite modest.

Even if these territorial figures are balanced out on the basis of differentiating between the Desert and the Sown, the results are much the same. Half of Israel was itself desert, and the experience of Israeli cultivation has shown what can be done to reclaim desert areas with irrigation. In view of the cheap fuel possible both for irrigation and for the desalting of the sea, it is plain that the historically desert areas of the Arab world, including the Sahara, could in principle be reclaimed without difficulty.

Thus it might have seemed entirely plausible—that is, historically and politically equitable—to regard the basic Zionist claim as realistic—that the true interests of the countries bordering Israel were not threatened and that the Arab states might fairly be expected eventually to accommodate the existence of a small non-Arab state in their midst.

This is, no doubt, the fundamental rationale for the emergence of the slogan of the "Palestinian people," so persuasive that it remains puzzling why it was not conceived long before the Six-day War of 1967. Why not at the very moment of the Israeli fight for independence in 1947 and 1948, when one might have thought it would spring into being, as it were, spontaneously?

For a few decades, of course, as the optimism—indeed, the euphoria—of the Arab leaders seemed to be soaring in spite of setbacks, there was no place for the notion of a "Palestinian people" (which did not, after all, exist). While the Arab leaders remained hopeful, at least rhetorically, there was no occasion to create a manifestly artificial "claim," since in the upsurge of self-consciousness attendant on the emancipation and eventual renovation of Arabdom, the intrusion of a small alien state, established moreover by a semipariah people, seemed both preposterous and offensive. It must have seemed that the "movement of history"—itself no doubt a myth—was simply against it, that it could not possibly last.

But as the morale and technology of the Israelis proved capable of both organizing a state and a seemingly first-class army, as the allegiance of American Jewry and the sponsorship of the United States remained constant, and as the Israelis emerged victorious from three peculiarly intense though brief wars, the public-relations element of the Arab resistance surfaced in force—made all the more potent by the role it could play in the venomous rivalries and intrigues of the Arab participants themselves.

Those intrigues are being played out, after all,

against a background of pervasive maladjustment, compounded of massive misery and illiteracy on one hand and fabulous oil resources in a few states on the other. The social problems afflicting the Arabic-speaking world as a whole naturally find their expression in politics and if, in Clausewitz's fashionable phrase, war itself is no more than a "continuation of politics by other means," it may be easy to find in the turmoil of the contemporary Arabic-speaking world an explanation of the peculiar Arab intransigence vis-à-vis Israel.

Unlike the deeply rooted problems of society, the problems presented by a war can often be solved; a government can whip up enthusiasm, rally its forces, and seem to be wielding authority with relative ease. A war enables a government to claim the resources of its partisans; it justifies countless "austerity" measures; it strengthens the executive; it concentrates power, with its collateral feeling of control. Thus, from an operational point of view, the temptation to keep its instruments tuned to a high pitch is potent. It is countered, in fact, only when the "reality principle" finally forces itself into practical affairs—that is, if the Egyptian army were really to be smashed openly, publicly, and unmistakably, the fundamental situation would be altered.

This highlights, of course, the fundamental dilemma of the Israeli leadership; for no matter how many battles they may win, it is clear they cannot actually intervene in the internal affairs of their neighbors. They cannot *govern* anyone else, probably not even through puppet governments. Hence, in a broad sense, even if they could conceivably eliminate the armies of their opponents, they could not create a situation in which they could prevent the formation of other armies.

This is why there is an element of plausibility in the statements by Arab spokesmen that "time is on their side." If the disproportion of the population figures (more than a hundred million Arabs against three million Israelis) is interpreted optimistically—granting a degree of cohesiveness, singleness of purpose, and homogeneity that may not exist—it means, quite simply, that the advantages of Israeli skill, devotion, and external support will ultimately be nullified.

It is just this preponderance in favor of the Arabs that in the minds of many outsiders makes it difficult to understand the intractability of the Arab leadership on the question of Palestine. It seems plain that the peculiar venom that infuses all discussions of the Israeli problem is ultimately derived from the ensemble of attitudes that weigh so heavily on the intelligentsias of the Middle East and the Third World as they confront their relationship with the West.

In terms of individual confrontation, the West is a broad and diffuse concept—it is so pervasive that it is not quite a reality. On the other hand, for the countries bordering Israel, the mythological projections of propaganda and resentment kindle the most violent passions. Thus, despite the closeness of Israel, which might be thought to make it somehow commonplace, despite the presence in Israel of a million Arabs, both resident and transient, the very idea of Israel can generate the most unbalanced diatribes.

The obduracy of the Arab leadership with respect to Israel has buttressed an interest often expressed in the West: Is there such a thing as the "Arab character"? Is it really an "enigma"?

In this domain clichés are, of course, rife. The Arabs have been thrust so insistently on the attention of the West because of the Israeli conflict that the combination of their unfamiliar history—as unfamiliar to them as to most Westerners!—and their present-day deportment has made them the embodiment of a wide variety of myths. The "irrational" elements in the contemporary Arab behavior seem to clamor for clarification. The clamor has created a mini-industry.

Attempting to "explain" the "Arab character," many Westerners resort to bizarrely capricious mixtures of theory and observation. The very fact that such portmanteau concepts as "Arab mind" can be used at all indicates, I suppose, the remoteness of the subject, if it is one; no one in his senses, after all, would talk about the "French mind" or the "Italian mind."

Many theorists resort to a peculiar combination of home-grown psychology—with a substantial admixture of vulgarized Freudianism—echoes of "tribal" elements in the Arab past, and the flashy rhetoric of intellectuals and propagandists. The notion of Arabs as governed, for instance, by a preoccupation with "shame," together with an obsession for "vengeance," is a seedbed for such "explanations." Obvious features of collective behavior such as conformity, honor, and solidarity are hypostatized, as it were, to become criteria for judging a social ethos that is claimed to be radically different from the behavior of other groups. This is, no doubt, the basis for the cliché that Arab society is "shame-oriented," in contradistinction to "Judeo-

Christian society"—"guilt-oriented." The role of
vengeance is, naturally, the cancellation of shame.

This may be helpful, to be sure, in explaining a
characteristic of Arab behavior much commented
on: the overemphasis on appearances and the value
placed on model behavior as opposed to real feeling, and on rhetoric as opposed to action.

Thus the inability of the Arab states to swallow
the fact of the existence of Israel may be said to be
due to a sense of the shame of defeat and a concomitant desire to wipe out the shame. The abolition of Israel would be seen as accomplishing a dual
objective: restoring the land wrongfully snatched
from the "Palestinians" and canceling the shame of
the massive defeats inflicted on so many Arabs by
so few Israelis.

It is commonplace among Arabs that rivals will
stop at nothing—"goal orientation" is a blanket
justification for anything. Thus political rivals will
quite unscrupulously use whatever issue they can in
order to look better than each other. This makes it
exceptionally difficult for any political candidate to
sound "weak" on Israel, or France, or Britain, or
the United States, or for that matter on any subject
governed by conformity—the charge of "betrayal"
would be automatic. This psychological factor
makes for a general pervasiveness of mistrust and
suspicion vis-à-vis all possible rivals, and indeed
with respect to everyone. It makes it easy for Arab
factions to maneuver against each other by cyni-
cally using against rivals the free-floating anxieties
and hostilities of the mob.

Consequently, even while generally accepted
shibboleths oblige Arab regimes to pledge total co-
operation with each other vis-à-vis Israel, at the

same time it is possible for them to evade the consequences of such declarations, or what in a Western milieu would be such consequences, by doing practically nothing. It is enough, because of an Arab preoccupation with forms instead of substance, to proclaim one's helpfulness rather than to implement it. This is no doubt a fundamental reason for the striking absence of cohesion among Arab allies whose public statements would lead outsiders to imagine the most intimate solidarity among them. At the same time, the *public* acknowledgment of a lack of solidarity would be regarded as a blow to the ideal of solidarity that is paid so much lip service.

Thus, if the Arabs are not, deep down, so *very* anti-Israel, there may still be hope for an ultimate accommodation.

To be sure, the appearances militating against this may have deeper roots after all. The rhetorical extravagance of the Arab spokesmen may not leave much latitude for optimism. Arab leaders have, for instance, made unstinting use of the "Protocols of the Elders of Zion," concocted in a French police department, exploited by the Tsarist government, and distributed on a massive scale by Hitler—and by Henry Ford in the twenties. This notorious forgery has been disseminated in tens of millions of copies both by Saudi Arabia and by Egypt.

It would certainly be hard to imagine anything more anti-Semitic than the "Protocols," founded upon the primordial concept of Christianity that the Jews, though seemingly helpless, are in reality engaged in a potent conspiracy to rule the world on behalf of Satan.

Arab leaders also showed remarkable energy in

the United Nations in the autumn of 1975, in securing the passage of the resolution denouncing Zionism as "racism." Externally, indeed, there would
seem to be no difference between the tactics of
contemporary Arab leaders and of classical anti-
Semites.

On the other hand, it would seem more reasonable, in spite of such evidence, to ascribe the extravagance of the anti-Israeli reaction to the hyper-
trophy of the rhetoric I have mentioned in
discussing the Arabic-speaking intelligentsia. The
rhetoric is obviously superficial just because it lacks
the foundation of anti-Semitism that in Christendom is endemic.

The notion that the Jews are a limb of Satan—
the linchpin of historic anti-Semitism—is entirely
missing in Islam, which merely looks down on Jews
as it does on all nonbelievers. Hence the "Protocols," though they *seem* to serve the same purpose
as they did for Hitler and Henry Ford, do no more
in the case of Muslim regimes than illustrate another cluster of themes—rhetorical overemphasis,
unscrupulousness, and irresponsibility.

In personal contacts between Arabs and Jews, for
instance, there is a basic harmony, even perhaps
amity. In London, Arabs and Jews are often per-
fectly friendly. Personal relations appear unrelated
to policy; no sensible English Jew would be
offended at being excluded from Saudi Arabia simply because he is a Jew. There is a sort of principle
involved, no doubt; the distribution of the "Protocols" means *something*. Yet without the fundamental thrust of the role played so potently in the
Christian psyche by the arch myth of anti-Semitism
—the satanic role of Jewry—the "Protocols" must

be interpreted as merely another form of propaganda, without deep roots in the unconscious.

The Egyptian-Israeli truce of 1975 may have been a turning point. The quarrel between Israel and Egypt, after all, was never very real from the point of view of the Egyptians, who for a millennium had shown no interest in the Arabic-speaking East. Large numbers of opinion-molding Egyptians, oppressed more and more frighteningly by the various miasmas of Egyptian life, may sincerely wish to make an honorable exit from the senseless imbroglio with Israel. They may allow their "mythical" perception of Israel to be molded by the ordinary processes of historical development, while contenting themselves in the here and now by dealing pragmatically with immediate issues.

But any basic settlement will have to depend on a deflection of the thrust of Soviet expansionism, or on the modification by the Soviet of its cosmic ambitions. The checkmate of the Soviet Government in Egypt has been met by the Soviet leaders with characteristic flexibility.

Though confused during the Lebanese civil war in 1975–76 by its simultaneous backing of factions that subsequently fell out—the PLO and the Assad regime—the Soviet leadership could easily accommodate the ascension of Syria as boss of the groups swirling along the northern borders of Israel. Picking its way carefully among the murderous rivalries of contending Arab power-centers, the Soviet leadership may still be able to use both Syria and Iraq, even Jordan, as stalking horses in the Middle East. The role of the PLO is not necessarily diminished: its disparate elements can easily be reshuffled to enable the organization as a whole to be presented to the world as the vanguard of the anti-Israeli coalition.

But it would be absurd to make specific forecasts. The "socialism" of the "radical" Arab states is a little theatrical; it too may be swept away or substantially modified by a new turn of events. The prospect of having the Soviet Union actually rooted on their own soil may eventually persuade not only the Saudi Arabians and the Iranians to set their face against Soviet intrusion, but the Iraqis and Syrians, too.

Thus against a perpetually changing background, rapprochement between Israel and its neighbors seems conceivable, if the vast forces involved tilt only slightly in a favorable direction.

OIL

The puzzles confronting the student of the Middle East have lately been given a new importance. The specific gravity of Arabdom in the world at large has been magnified by the oil weapon.

Oil made its debut as an ostensible political factor during the Yom Kippur War of 1973. For the first time, the oil kings and sheiks of the Arabian Peninsula, in control of resources that could exercise a direct effect on the world economy as a whole—especially Western Europe and Japan, and even the United States—moved ostentatiously into a commanding position. They proclaimed an oil embargo that would be mitigated or canceled only if their political demands, revolving around the claims of the "Palestinian people," were met.

It is true that the oil embargo, coupled immediately as it was with a general raising of prices, quickly proved to be no embargo at all, but merely an economic squeeze intended to make respectable an old-fashioned commercial ploy; the political overtones were obviously secondary. Nevertheless, by revealing to a broad public for the first time just what the oil resources of the Arab world amounted to, and by presenting the message in a broadly conceived package entailing the concept of a "Palestinian Arab" people, the engineers of the ploy produced a profound effect. Their political bombshell had a marked impact not only on the evolution of the negotiations set in train by the Yom Kippur War but also on the economy of the world.

While dramatically effective when injected into international politics and economics, the oil weapon has obvious limitations—mainly of time. Technicians all over the world have long been aware that the fossil fuels now supporting the world economy are ultimately bound to run out, and have been striving to come up with alternative sources of energy. The effort expended in this direction has merely been intensified since 1973. Whatever the present shortcomings of the various possibilities already adumbrated—atomic energy, solar energy, geothermal energy, and wind energy, to mention a few—they seem destined to solve the basic problem of energy in the near future, a span of time perhaps to be reckoned not in decades, but in years.

No doubt it was the awareness of this eventuality that prompted the oil princes of the Persian Gulf area, including one of the major producers, Iran, to concert their efforts during the Yom Kippur War. They hoped to secure a maximum economic advantage, and in the case of the Arab producers a sort of political fringe benefit from the financial squeeze.

The oil embargo of 1973–74 gave rise to a fear that the concentration of vast oil revenues in the hands of a small number of people might upset the industrial world, that the manipulation of literally tens of billions of dollars by a few individuals acting as a unit might tilt the world economy in one way or another. This was felt with all the greater force since it seemed inconceivable for such huge sums to be invested at home; there is scarcely anything like the infrastructure needed to absorb such sums: Vast, expert intelligentsias will have to be created practically *ex nihilo;* indeed, in the case of all Arab countries but Egypt the population as a whole is far too exiguous to play a role in the foreseeable future. There is no immediately effective way, in short, of implementing large-scale investment.

It is the absence of any real industry in any of these countries—even in Iran, the most extensive and cultivated—that made it natural for the oil producers to harmonize their efforts in a crash program intended to secure enough liquid funds to establish a financial base for both profitable investment in the industrial economy of the West and, ideally, the creation of a bona fide industrial plant in their own lands. It is the ominous feeling that time is working *against* them that no doubt fuels the somewhat frenetic thrust for a global solution to the economic problems confronting the Middle East as a whole.

Nevertheless, oil revenues have been partially invested in building up the home plant, even in the wilderness of Saudi Arabia, and the rest have been scattered around the world investment market, politically denatured, as it were, en route, and absorbed into the torrent of liquid capital on a short-term basis or else invested, to a much smaller degree, in large-scale institutional projects. The Arabs have already lost whatever political goal might have been attributed to them, and are simply following the guidelines laid down by sober accountancy.

Thus the magnitude of the capital sums now in the hands of the oil potentates, so alarming at the outset, has already been discounted; the plutocracy of the world has grown by one more segment. If anything, the concentration of the capital in the hands of a few coteries in the Persian Gulf has already had a perhaps predictable effect on politics. If the informal anti-Soviet accord reached among Iran, Saudi Arabia, and Egypt has transcended the Israeli problem by a realignment in terms of the real relationships among great powers, it may be taken as the harbinger of a new and statesmanlike appreciation of the true proportions of things. The Middle East may be integrated in the world economy on its own terms after all.

What has already been accomplished, in any case, at least in its initial stages, is the maturing of a new type of Arab intellectual, quite different from the flashy levantines I mentioned before.

With the flow of money from the oil resources of so many Arab states, the need for business managers, bureaucrats, and practical intellectuals to handle affairs in their countries has produced a competent corps of experts.

Tens of thousands of young people during the past quarter century have made their way through the university systems of France, Great Britain, the United States, and Germany. Looking essentially for a technical education, and hence favoring great training centers like the Harvard Business School, they have effected the transition from the old-fashioned societies of their origin to the modern ethos of the West.

Hence it is commonplace to meet entirely urbane Arabs in positions of authority in all the worldwide institutions that have been proliferating since the Second World War. These positions of authority, moreover, have latterly been increasing in direct ratio to the preponderance of oil as a factor in world trade. The economic integration of the Middle East in world trade has, in short, found its natural expression in movements of personnel.

These urbane Arabs—economists, business managers, engineers, even public-relations men!—seem to have nothing "Arab" about them except, occasionally, their traditional dress, emphasized sometimes in order to make an impression on Westerners. In fact, the discarding of the traditional garb, which is also quite practical, for the trappings of the Western executive would itself be a form of snobbery, an insecure way of responding to the West. That form of insecurity is surely bound to change radically as the Arab world plays an increasingly important role in guiding its own destinies.

VII

The Prospect

It seems undeniable that the ordeal of the Western experience has given rise to a spiritual crisis throughout Islam—most intense, perhaps, in the Arabic-speaking world.

Itself quintessentially a parallel elaboration of the same legacy that underlies Western society—a mélange of Judaism and Hellenism—Islam nevertheless transformed that legacy in its own way: On the basis of the same amalgam it produced an idiosyncratic society that was never subjected to an all-out onslaught until a few generations ago.

At its very inception, to be sure, Muhammad's cluster of basic ideas came up against the Middle East as a whole, but Muslim arms were so successful against the feeble defenses of Byzantium and Persia that practically overnight the civilization of the Middle East was engulfed wholesale. Only then did Islam become Islam.

The whole process took place so rapidly, so unconsciously, that most subjects of the new empire

had no occasion to realize that Islam had been filled
up with foreign content and only then covered
with a Muslim veneer. The first Muslim Arabs had
in any case been indifferent to the ideas of their
subjects, and a few generations later, Hellenist and
Persian ideas had already been digested. Soulless artifacts and techniques were absorbed without
awareness; some basic mental habits, Greek in origin but universal in application—logic, theory,
science—could be assimilated without friction; but
the ideal view that had infused Greek civilization in
its totality was discarded.

Later on, the religion evolved into a ramified
structure with a massive intellectual and dogmatic
anchorage superimposed on its Hellenistic legacy.
Grounded now in material assimilated from the
Hellenistic milieu but organically integrated, Muslim orthodoxy resisted perceptibly foreign ideas
with deep mistrust; further imports from Christendom were combated as being disturbingly alien.
The resistance to ideas that characterized Islam at
its height and during its decline—from A.D. 850 to
1400—was ultimately to warp Muslim perspective.

For centuries Europe was inferior to Islam in all
respects. Then, after the Ottoman Turks established themselves in southeastern Europe, they
served as a great barrier against the manifold
influences of the West. But as the Turks were
dislodged from their foothold in Europe, and as
Western Europe, reinforced by the discovery of
the New World and the great trade routes to India
and the Far East, began its massive spread throughout the world, once again Islam was forced in on itself, competing, manifestly, not with an altogether
alien culture, but precisely with another variant of

its own culture. Essentially this was at worst a civil war situation, at best an exchange of ideas within a unitary area of civilization, an area delineated by the common heritage of Greek thought, Roman law, a revealed monotheism, and a fusion of philosophy and theology. Though each side was perhaps too close to its own preoccupations to see the wood for the trees, both had a common spiritual background that was, perhaps, just what made intercommunication so irritating.

Today the whole of Islam, its Arabic-speaking segment in the forefront, is confronting the West in a far more self-conscious way. Reborn in many respects ever since its rise to self-consciousness a couple of generations ago, the Arab world is still in a thoroughly inferior position, both intellectually and materially. At the same time it has a fund of indigenous strength to draw on.

The confrontation between the Arab world and the modern West is, after all, complex. The cosmic rivalries of the United States, the Soviet Union, and China provide a framework spacious enough, and at the same time flexible enough for small centers of power to find numerous points of support.

A vast and largely unconscious accommodation, to be sure, has already been made. State administration in practically all the states now calling themselves "Arab" has been sweepingly overhauled on European models. This particular adaptation to Europe, perhaps because it was one of the technical artifacts that can migrate freely without arousing spiritual malaise, spread by a sort of osmosis very rapidly without attracting, as it were, any notice.

Egypt especially, no doubt the cultural leader of the Arab world, is fundamentally European in all

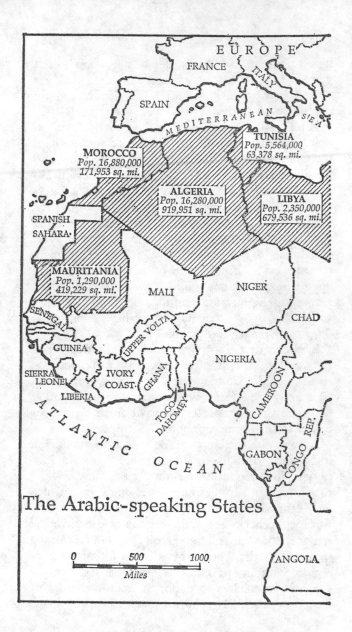

The Arabic-speaking States

MOROCCO
Pop. 16,880,000
171,953 sq. mi.

TUNISIA
Pop. 5,564,000
63,378 sq. mi.

ALGERIA
Pop. 16,280,000
919,951 sq. mi.

LIBYA
Pop. 2,350,000
679,536 sq. mi.

MAURITANIA
Pop. 1,290,000
419,229 sq. mi.

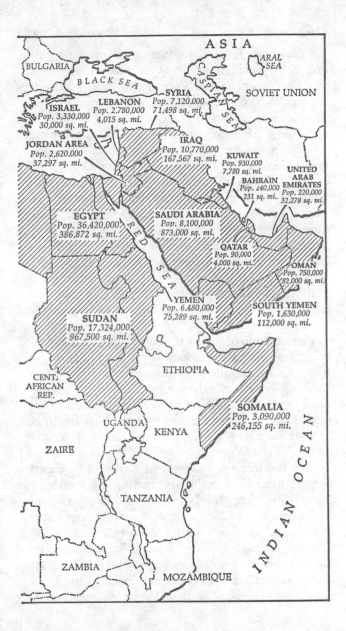

basic aspects. Even the government preceding the present regime launched by Nasser in 1953 was modeled more on the French absolutist monarchs than on the Turkish executive. This is so even now, since its administration and the economy stem from a mingling of European socialist ideas and capitalism. Even the ancient University of Al-Azhar, the venerable Muslim divinity school (founded around 972), has been reorganized along the lines of a Western university combined with elementary instruction. When the Nasser regime abolished Egypt's legal subordination to the European communities and at the same time eliminated its Western constitutional and representative democracy, it merely introduced a cluster of still other European institutions—the authoritarian, quasitotalitarian pattern now being adopted by other Arabic-speaking countries as well.

The example of Japan is enlightening. If the Japanese, an entirely non-European people to begin with, could assimilate Western technology while retaining their own ethos, why should it be impossible for a culturally similar civilization like Islam to take over European achievements, digest them in its own way, and be transformed into another extension of the West?

The Westernizing movement has already wiped out the main element in the traditional societies of the Middle East and North Africa—the powerful land-owning minority—whose hold on vast stretches of land has been for many centuries the cardinal socio-economic factor. The landed elite has been shouldered aside by a two-pronged social drive, comprised of both the middle-class entrepreneurs, modeled on their Western counterparts, and the world-reform movements, modeled even more closely on the socialist movements of the West. In a number of countries—Egypt, Libya, Syria, Iraq, Algeria, and Tunisia—socialist movements have either eliminated or shackled the land owners and, for that matter, of course, the middle-class entrepreneurs, too.

The mere enumeration of what is required for the Europeanization of a non-European power demonstrates the ineluctability of the process. If a country wants a defense force, it must get it from those who can build defense forces; if it wants economic independence, it needs industrialization and massive investment; even to achieve independence in the arts and sciences, essential nowadays for psychological self-assurance, it is the West that must be studied and translated.

Just because Islam has always been considered by Muslims the final religion, they find it difficult to regard it as merely one among many civilizations whose differences naturally produce different values. Muslims tend to look at other societies from the point of view of the degree of nearness to or remoteness from Islam.

By and large, Muslims are remarkably ignorant of the evolution of Islam. Indeed, the fruitful inquiries of the past hundred years into the early history of Islam have been carried out by Europeans. The results have not yet been adequately transmitted to Muslim youth, partly, no doubt, because of the radically defective educational system and partly because of the shattering effect the society as a whole has been subjected to by the collision with the West.

It is just this disorientation that has accentuated

the pivotal role of the intelligentsia. However restive, alarming, and troublesome the headstrong new intelligentsias may be, their minds teeming passionately with various half-baked formulations of fashionable socio-economic panaceas, they are the repository, for good or ill, of vital educational and administrative capacities. In the Middle East, more particularly, they are the channels and the exponents of the "national idea" that has taken possession, as it seems, of the elite as a whole.

Those undergoing cultural shock cannot survey their situation with detachment. Their basic motivation in "justifying themselves" is essentially apologetic. Thus modern Arabs, awakening to the dynamic turbulence of the twentieth century, are bound to reassess their own past vis-à-vis the West, especially when talking to Westerners but also even when speaking among themselves. They must pull themselves up by their bootstraps, breaking out of their own cultural tradition—whose vehicle is, naturally, the educational system, notoriously difficult to reform—and force themselves to cope with realities.

It is no more than natural for them to hark back to a period when Islam was turning sterile, when style was cultivated for its own sake, when rhetoric, however empty, was endlessly refined. To this day, indeed, an emphasis on words in contrast with execution seems to many observers a feature of the Arabic-speaking intelligentsia. The dualism involved in fusing rhetorical exuberance with executive futility torments all those Arab intellectuals who really would like to *do* something, but are hamstrung by a tradition that is content with its self-involved futility.

It is more convenient to take refuge in sweeping generalities that enable them to put shortcomings and incapacities in the most favorable light—in creating caricatures, for instance, of the "spiritual" East as contrasted with the "materialist" West.

Nothing is easier, to be sure, than to demonstrate that the hoary cliché about an irreconcilable antagonism between East and West is altogether superficial, indeed silly and merely ignorant. But the ordeal of modernization, just because it involves areas of deep insecurity, is painful. Islam, and *a fortiori* the Arabic-speaking world in its van, still balks at acknowledging—even recognizing—the intellectual spirit underlying its technological acquisitions from the West. Just because Arabdom still feels hard-pressed, it is concerned for its spiritual core.

Yet while an identity of heritage in Islam and Christendom is obvious, there are numerous specific obstacles to the integration of the contemporary Arabic-speaking elite with the Western world.

Perhaps the outstanding contradiction today between traditional Muslim attitudes and the West is the concept of progress. A self-sufficient universe, Islam regards all truths as inherited from an ideal past; there is no need to add to them—that would contradict the theory of self-sufficiency. It has been the traditional Muslim view that the world has been deteriorating at least from the time of Muhammad. A seemingly fundamental attitude, it is deeply rooted in Muslim society as the heir of Hellenism, which like so many other societies had also looked back to a golden age, and could be maintained even in the face of what seemed to be incontrovertible evidence to the contrary. In the ninth and tenth centuries A.D., for instance, Islam soared to a zenith never equaled since. Nevertheless, during this protracted age, when not only literature and science were making great leaps forward, but the political power of the realm itself was also expanding steadily, it remained a commonplace that each successive age was inevitably inferior to its predecessors.

Linked to an inherent depression and nostalgia, this world view was reinforced by real events as the Caliphate began "decaying" and the somewhat mindless conformism that characterized the later medieval period was buttressed by the collateral view that man had nothing better to do than to go on repeating *ad infinitum* the accomplishments of predecessors. Fostered by education and the accumulation of tradition, this Muslim attitude of inertia is plainly a barrier to any initiative on behalf of large-scale reforms.

Moreover, both in the spirit of the state and in the ethos of modern societies, Islam has negative elements. The notions that in the West have been taken for granted since the French Revolution—democracy and curbs on the executive—are alien to Middle Eastern tradition.

It is true, as we have seen, that democracy is at the heart of Islam, entailed in the idea of the equality of human beings as children of the One God. Yet the *de facto* evolution of Islam for the past millennium, plus the philosophy (juristic and otherwise) devised to accommodate the historical facts, has so overlaid the democracy implied by monotheism and by the free-and-equal life of the Bedouin who carried the seeds of Islam abroad, that the democratic ideal has become entirely fossilized, something to be paid mere lip service.

This is further accentuated by the radical failure of Islam during the past millennium to evolve a parallel to the humanism that with time overcame the institutional freezing of medieval Christianity. Whereas Christendom ultimately worked out of its inner core a humanistic development to counteract its topheavy, life-denying theology, Islam, with the same heritage, never gave the ideal of democracy a genuine intellectual underpinning.

Another obstacle in the creation of an administrative ethos—summed up as a feeling that governments are somehow meant to represent the interests of the community as a whole—has been the general pessimism of Islam with respect to government as such.

In the light of the decay that since the days of the Envoy has been ineluctable, it has been natural for Muslims to be cynical about the very institution of government. In traditional Islam civic-mindedness would have been intellectually and emotionally absurd: The pious have tended to hold themselves aloof from the state. While the executive obviously had to be obeyed, both from the point of view of law as such as well as from that of common sense, it was accepted among believers that the dispositions taken by the rulers were either unlawful at worst and at best outside the domain of the religious sanctions that in Islam were held to underlie *true* government.

Islamic law in and for itself has nothing to say about restricting the sovereign's powers, still less about any form of consulting the community at large in the manner of parliamentary democracy, though there are modernists, to be sure, who insist on interpreting a few phrases wrenched out of con-

text from the Quran and made to authorize constitutional reform as a return to the primeval purity
of God-given Islam.

Yet even a cursory glance at the context indicates
that their being singled out illustrates no more than
a traditional Muslim proclivity for finding sanction
for anything in the Quran.

A further pitfall for an Arab growing up in the
modern era is the conflict between traditional allegiances to family, clan, and sect, and the new allegiances now required in one way or another by the
state.

Muslims traditionally have been wrapped in such
local allegiances, which did not collide at any point
with the religious core of Islam. In Islam, which
never mediated salvation, religious feeling remained
as in Protestantism a personal matter: Believers had
to settle accounts with their Maker as best they
could. Yet the pervasive role of the modern state
has now imposed on Muslim Arabs a whole set of
novel requirements that transcend all local and personal attachments. The modern state demands more
from Muslims than Islam without finding anything
in Muslim tradition to buttress those demands.

At the same time, though the ensemble of Western culture has descended on Islam, a certain
amount of selectivity, at least in emphasis, has been
inevitable. The conflicts within that selectivity
seem endless. Since the West has been presented to
Islam mainly through its technology and political
predominance, there is no way for Western values
proper to be digested or even, perhaps, understood.
Arabs throbbing with xenophobia will simultaneously be infatuated by countless aspects of Western culture. They find themselves leading very

different lives at home and in public, since family life is bound to be outpaced by technological readjustment.

Oddly enough, the one fundamental idea developed by the West that has been authentically digested by all Islam is Darwin's theory of evolution. It has been assimilated, no doubt, not so much because of its intellectual seductiveness as because of the purely sociopolitical hope it offers a decadent Arab world for its own regeneration. It provides a proof, so to speak, that the inferior status of Arabdom and Islam as a whole is not fixed but is, on the contrary, in the very midst of upheaval and change.

The evolutionary notion is plastic enough to fit in with the determinism that is otherwise a pervasive mood in Islam. Though the idea of fatalism—familiar to the West in the word "kismet"—has been frequently invoked by Muslims as a rationalization of behavior, it is obvious that it can rationalize any behavior at all, including dynamic, positive action. Thus Darwinism is a happy combination of free will and predestination.

Modern Muslim writers, hypnotized by the collision with the West and seeking points of support, are fond of talking up the great value of the Muslim unity between clergy and government—the Islamic equivalent of church and state. Yet it would seem that that unity is essentially obscurantist; it bars the advance of modern ideas.

In the West, after all, the Christian church, because of its profoundly antirational principles (Incarnation, redemptive Crucifixion, Resurrection—that is, the magical ensemble embedded in Christianity), was bound to be systematically obscurantist;

modern thought could advance only by rebelling *against* the Church, a rebellion that was at least facilitated by the division *de facto* between church and state. The fusion of the two in Islam therefore makes modernity far more vulnerable to the old-fashioned attitudes of the religious savants. Hence it would seem plain that, insofar as modern Muslims choose to identify Islam with its ecclesiastical component, to that extent they will be taking on an additional burden. They will have to establish their world view on a mythically reorganized traditional groundwork, since the historical groundwork would prove antithetical to any form of modern enlightenment.

Contrariwise, the more modern Muslims look back to the core of their religion, without paying much attention to the massive encrustation imposed on it by history, the more they will be able to apply the traditional method of adaptation to the sacred book—simple "reinterpretation," a potently flexible device.

Nothing is easier, for instance, than to find in the Quran a prohibition of polygamy—if one knows how to look—even though it might be thought the Quran explicitly allows a man to marry not merely one woman, but two, three, or four, if he thinks he can deal with them justly. Elsewhere, however, the Quran says that no one can be *really* just, and since just treatment of all four wives is expressly demanded, it can be shown quite easily that the Quran, by demanding an impossible justice, actually enforces monogamy!

Thus the choice is still open-ended. Muslim Arabs, like Muslims in general, will be able to go back to what is construed as the true core; by a

simple, sensible, and indeed logical and morally persuasive method they could easily reinterpret the
Quran as a book of humanist guidelines. If the
spirit of the law rather than its letter is set up as the
criterion, it will be simple to shed the countless
juristic and socio-economic encrustations as obso-
lete. It is really a question of applying to the Quran
the endless potential inherent in all interpretation,
thus enabling the emancipated or semi-emancipated
Muslim of today to retain a maximum amount of
his own culture, which in spite of all secular-mind-
edness he doubtless wishes to do. It will make it
possible to introduce a certain amount of criticism
into the attitude toward authority, and thus facili-
tate the acceptance of Western realities—that is,
science. Modern Muslims must become aware, in
short, both of the conflict between traditional and
present-day attitudes, and of the possibilities of
overcoming the conflict by the use of indigenous
material. In this respect, indeed, it would be more
sensible for Muslim reformers to emphasize, as
grounds for hopefulness, just what distinguishes
Islam from Christendom—the absence of an organized church distinct from the community at large.

The contradictory relationship between Muslim
initiative and Muslim dependence is present in all
realms—scholarship, art, literature, and, most painful of all, in education, where far-reaching decisions must constantly be made. In the very midst of
creating a new life for a renovated society it will be
plain to the reformers that their inspiration comes
from abroad; all the impetuousness in the world
will not make it easy for the young men who play
so massive a role in the Arab world to effect a reconciliation between two ways of life that, however

much their origins have in common, are felt to be somehow antagonistic. Neither tradition—that of Islam nor that of the West—can be simply dropped, especially since the inferiority generally ascribed to Islam vis-à-vis Western techniques makes Muslims hypersensitive about borrowings they are obliged to make. Thus Arabs become hypersensitive about clinging to their own ideals precisely at a point when those ideals are being downgraded by the manifest superiority of the West.

The dream of ardent Muslims is a simple one—to build a modern state on the basis of Islam. In principle this is entirely feasible. Islam, properly understood, is so simple that it cannot be said to conflict with any aspect of modernity—except, perhaps, a "scientific" approach to the Quran!—but there are so many emotional obstacles that in the spirit of any given individual a painful conflict is likely to rage.

For Christian Arabs, to be sure, the process is infinitely simpler both psychologically and, as it were, technically. Christian Arabs have *already* been Westernized, either by Roman Catholicism or by Greek Orthodoxy, and to a small extent by Protestantism. It is one of the reasons, as we have seen, why it was Christians who kindled Arab nationalism to begin with; it has also been easier, perhaps, for Christians, against a Muslim background, to take to Marxism—an even more sweeping panacea than nationalism and massively buttressed by foci of power abroad.

The identity of each individual country in the Arab world, as well as the identity of Islam itself, can only be strengthened by its immersion in Western ideas. The danger of losing identity—a claim frequently made by old-fashioned critics warning against Western influence—was a danger only when the Arab world was not strong enough to withstand such influences. With the authority arising out of the awareness of their own past, Arabs will eventually have no difficulty defending themselves spiritually.

Religion, the chief area in which old-fashioned Muslims are still apprehensive about the corrupting influences of the West, will always be there to serve as a bulwark against foreign atheism.

GLOBAL PERSPECTIVES

All these civic considerations have been, to be sure, largely superseded—as they have in the West —by the formula of totalitarianism, which in many ways bypasses the conflicts outlined above.

It is true that dictatorship on the modern—communist—pattern can hardly be said to exemplify any Islamic principle; on the other hand, for those Muslims who are inclined to wash their hands of any responsibility for modern government, the combination of coercion and corruption characteristic of such a dictatorship makes it easy for them to do so. From another point of view, it enables the partisans of dictatorship themselves to feel a self-righteous composure by carrying out, as members of a small, self-authorized elite, all the reforms they feel society is crying for. It provides a conspiratorial allegiance that in many ways replaces the traditional allegiances to clan and family, and at the same time invests this allegiance with a global and pansocial aura.

The churning-up so obvious nowadays has been in effect for more than a century. The collision with the West, which has already transformed all social, spiritual, and political life throughout the world, has had the same effect—indeed, even more so—on Islam. It has led, no doubt predictably, to the resurgence of positive willpower in all the great nations that went through the mangling machine of Western innovations. In the case of the Arabs, a substantial segment of Islam, it has re-created, in a profound sense, a feeling of nationhood among peoples whose only common attribute before the modern period, for more than a millennium, was the mere possession of a common tongue.

In the space of only a generation or two, the Arabic-speaking peoples, benefiting, of course, by the countless weaknesses, rivalries, competitions, and frictions in the West, have formed themselves into a self-conscious community that, even though split up into twenty small nation-states, is nevertheless showing, very gradually, a will not only to survival, but also to an increasingly active role in the management of its own affairs. The struggle of the self-conscious elements—dedicated in unequal portions to nationalism, conservatism, and/or reformism with respect to the Islamic past, and most recently to Marxism and other forms of socialism—has been to resist the West as far as possible, while at the same time curbing or stifling those aspects of indigenous tradition that are hampering the struggle.

The rapid shifts of mood that characterize the Arab intelligentsia, and that have nowhere been so apparent as in the long-drawn-out struggle with the small State of Israel, may now finally be diminishing, to be replaced by a more homogeneous, sober, and constructive mood—a composure derived from the emergence of the area as a whole into the international arena as a self-confident and influential factor, and also, of course, by the stimulation of the oil money.

The lopsidedness inherent in the present-day revival of Islam is apparent. Any outsider is aware that success in modernizing Islam is really more of a success in the political transformation of specific states rather than in a deep-rooted change of mind entailed by a genuine psychic transfiguration. In a sense, of course, this is what is meant by the greater ease of importing artifacts rather than spiritual values. Political institutions, in a way, are devices that can be transferred from society to society without bringing about changes in depth.

For the past century Islam has been fighting a rear-guard action. In our own day it is just this feeling of disadvantage, of external envy and suspiciousness pervading all aspects of the cultural flow from West to East that is psychologically so disturbing for many Arabs. This is especially true, perhaps, for those who have been receiving so thorough an education lately in the great capitals of the West.

In all probability, we are now witnessing the final stage in the homogenization of Islam and the West. As tens of thousands (soon, no doubt, hundreds of thousands) of Arabs continue streaming to London, Paris, and Massachusetts for an education in Western technology, management, and the humanities, to that extent they will be making a still further import of Western culture, in doses that will be both more massive and more concentrated. Since they will have been detached to some extent from their native roots—say, in the "Arabic sciences"—in order to make the cultural leap to begin with, they will be bridging in their own persons the chasm between Islam, still essentially medieval-minded, and the glittering world of the West.

They will thus be re-creating in their own persons an amalgam—Arab origins plus Western culture; it will not be a symbiosis except in that sense, since for the generation after them—assuming what is likely, that by then all present-day Western culture will have been transplanted linguistically into Arabic as well as implanted in the psyches of countless Arabs—very nearly the sum total of all culture will either be out-and-out Western, or Western with a tincture of Islam in what is outwardly professed.

There will be the usual spectrum of reactions characteristic of socio-intellectual convulsions: At one end fundamentalists will cling to the Quran—that is, to ancient interpretations of the Quran; at the other many will accept modern interpretations; in the middle—no doubt the largest sector—there will be those more or less indifferent to the whole question.

Anchored massively in a huge segment of the world's population, including Arabdom, Islam is scarcely likely to be wiped out physically; it is even less likely to lose its individuality, since it will be possible to impose its own essence on the mélange of Western ideas and institutions it will ultimately be steeped in.

In the quarter century since the Second World War, the Arab peoples of the Middle East and North Africa have manifested a lively reaction in politics; it is easy to see that it is much livelier than any parallel display of cultural self-individuation. But it would be misleading to overestimate the significance of the contrast, and surely a mistake to jump to the conclusion that the self-consciousness of the Arab world has already been annihilated.

It is only natural for the first reaction of a given society to be precisely on the administrative plane; it is no more than another and more extreme instance of the reform of the army defenses that historically has always been the first reform generated by a foreign threat. Once the societies involved respond by extruding a new carapace to take the blows of the external world, they will have time, underneath, to complete the true process of assimilation.

From a certain point of view it is bound to be disappointing to sympathetic students of Islam and Arabdom that the cultural reaction to the impact of the West so far has been at best mediocre. With such a reservoir of brainpower, the self-respect of an ancient identity, and a solid culture to draw on, the peoples grouped together now as Arabs might well have been expected to perform more dramatically. Indeed, it is very strange that even the great trail-blazing reinterpretation of the Muslim past is the handiwork of Western scholarship.

Yet such carping may be a mere by-product of our own timebound point of view. Who can foretell how long such a complex process requires to work itself out? The tardiness of attitudinal change —a form of psychic lag—may simply be the organism's self-defense, even though it no doubt detracts from the benefits that might otherwise accompany a genuinely fruitful borrowing. It may be con-

ceived of as a network of shoals contrived to safeguard the shoreline against the onslaught of too
many psychic elements advancing too quickly.

Now that we have at least partially overcome our
recent hyperrational tradition, we can see the decisive role that the unconscious is bound to play: Behavior is more intractable than institutions.

Arabdom has not yet perfected its response to
the West. Arabdom's stance is still polemical—
indeed, overpolemical. It is still learning, though
without an interior acceptance of the common
sense implied by that. Pride and suspicion, hall-
marks of weakness, still predominate.

The vast oil resources of the Middle East, whose
greater part is by quirk of circumstance in the
hands of the most backward Arab groups and
whose staggering magnitude has still to be digested,
have already performed an important function in
exacerbating the contrast between traditional inertia and a dynamic renovation of social outlook.
Affluence may overcome the somewhat defiant imi-
tativeness seemingly engrained in the current generation of opinion molders. The tensions of our
epoch, which solicit discipline, patience, and imagination, and a new view of social interaction, as
well as a more ample projection of collective ambitions, may vanish as the inflammation inflicted by
the West on the Arab psyche gradually dies down,
and Arabdom achieves true spiritual equality.

There are signs, indeed, that the reacquisition of
morale—a welcoming awareness of one's roots—
may be about to be consummated. Behind all the
ideological fashions that have been described—
socialism, communism, nationalism, democracy, totalitarianism—a stark and disconcerting element has

been looming up, both novel and age-old—the kindling of Muslim fervor.

Uniformly underestimated by superficial observers, this element of old-fashioned religiosity is nevertheless arrestingly obvious. In the recent convulsions of the Middle East—the conflict with Israel, the smashing of Lebanon, the deployment of oil money—we are witnessing not merely the play of worldly forces, not merely the resurgence of more or less Europeanized Arabs, but a resurgence of Islam as such. Western though the technological baggage of Islam may be, countless Muslims have already absorbed enough Western substance to begin acting out their desires in wholly religious terms. Headstrong and militant, Islam is on the march again.

Islam is not only a relatively unitary social sphere —its cosmic spraddle from the Atlantic Ocean through the heart of Siberia and Africa as far as India, Indonesia, and China makes it a unifying force in the world. If human adaptability is, as it seems, endlessly protean, Arabdom may prove to be a capacious reservoir for creative change. Together with its Christian component it is the vanguard of Islam, and in our own day it may make a contribution of its own that will re-create and amplify the role of its illustrious past.

Bibliography

Antonius, George, *The Arab Awakening*, New York, 1939.

Arnold, Sir Thomas, and Guillaume, Alfred (eds.), *The Legacy of Islam*, Oxford, 1931.

Becker, C. H., *Islamstudien*, Vols. I and II, Leipzig, 1924, 1932.

——, *Educational Problems in the Near East and the Far East*, London, 1933.

Bell, Richard, *Introduction to the Quran*, Edinburgh, 1953.

Brockelmann, Carl, *History of the Islamic Peoples*, New York, 1944.

Brunschvig, R., and Grunebaum, G. E. von (eds.), *Classicisme et Déclin Culturel*, Paris, 1957.

Burton, Richard, *A Pilgrimage to al-Medina and Mecca*, London, 1893.

Cahen, Claude, *Leçons d'Histoire Musulmane*, Paris, 1961.

Chelhod, Joseph, *Introduction à la Sociologie de l'Islam*, Paris, 1958.

Doughty, Charles, *Wanderings in Arabia Deserta*, London, 1888.

Farès, Bishr, "Difficultés pour un Ecrivain Arabe Moderne," *Revue des Etudes Islamiques*, Vol. X, 1936.

Faris, Nabih Amin (ed.), *The Arab Heritage*, New York, 1963.

Gabrieli, Francesco, *The Arab Revival*, New York, 1961.

——, *A Short History of the Arabs*, London, 1963.

Gardet, Louis, *La Cité Musulmane*, Paris, 1961.

Gibb, Sir Hamilton, *Studies on the Civilization of Islam*, London, 1962.

——, *Studies in Contemporary Arabic Literature*, Vols. 4, 5, and 7, *Bulletin of the School of Oriental Studies*, London.

—— (ed.), *Whither Islam?*, London, 1932.

Gibb, Sir Hamilton, and Bowen, Harold, *Islamic Society and the West*, Vol. I, London, 1957.

Goitein, S. D., *Jews and Arabs*, New York, 1955.

——, *Studies in Islamic History and Institutions*, Leiden, 1966.

Goldziher, Ignaz, *Muhammedanische Studien*, Vols. I and II, Halle an der Saale, 1888, 1890.

——, *Vorlesungen über den Islam*, Heidelberg, 1925.

Grunebaum, G. E. von, *Islam*, London, 1955.

Guillaume, Alfred, *Islam*, London, 1954.

Haim, Sylvia G. (ed.), *Arab Nationalism*, Los Angeles, 1964.

Hurgronje, Snouck, *Verspreide Geschriften*, Leipzig, 1923.

——, *Mohammedanism*, New York, 1916.

Husayn, Taha, *Fi al-Aql al-Arabi al-Hadith* (in a special number of *al-Hilal: al-Arab wa-l-Islam*), Cairo, 1939.

Junge, Reinhard, *Die Europäisierung orientalischer Wirtschaft*, Vol. I, E. Weimar, 1915.

Kohn, Hans, *Western Civilization in the Near East*, New York, 1936.

——, *Nationalism and Imperialism in the Hither East*, London, 1932.

——, *Die nationale Bewegung in Aegypten,* Zeitschrift für Politik, 1926.

——, *Der arabische Nationalismus,* Zeitschrift für Politik, 1927.

Krachkovsky, I., *Vozniknovenie i Razvitie novo-arabskoi literatury,* Vostok, Leningrad, 1922.

Lewis, Bernard, *The Arabs in History,* London, 1950.

Massignon, Louis, "Eléments arabes et Foyers d'Islamisation," *Revue du Monde Musulman,* Vol. 57, 1924.

Nicholson, Reynold A., *A Literary History of the Arabs,* Cambridge, 1930.

Nolte, Richard H. (ed.), *The Modern Middle East,* New York, 1963.

O'Leary, De Lacy, *How Greek Science Passed to the Arabs,* London, 1949.

Philby, H. St. John, *Arabia,* London, 1930.

——, *Harun al Rashid,* London, 1933.

Spuler, Bertold, *The Muslim World,* Vols. I and II, Leiden, 1960.

Sykes, Christopher, *Crossroads to Israel,* New York, 1965.

Toynbee, A. J., *A Study of History,* Vols. I, II, and III, London, 1934.

——, *The World After the Peace Conference,* London, 1925.

——, *Survey of International Affairs,* London, 1925.

Walzer, Richard, *Greek into Arabic,* Oxford, 1962.

University of Chicago, *Near East: Problems and Prospects,* Chicago, 1942.

PERIODICALS

al-Hilal, Cairo   *Koloniale Rundschau*
al-Muqtataf, Cairo   *Hochland*
Foreign Affairs   *Welt des Islams*
Round Table   *Revue des Etudes Islamiques*
Der Islam   *Revue du Monde Musulman*
Oriente Moderno   *Vostok*
Africa

Index